A NATURALIST'S G

BUTTERFLIES
OF
THE PHILIPPINES

Jade Aster T. Badon

JOHN BEAUFOY PUBLISHING

First published in the United Kingdom in 2023 by John Beaufoy Publishing Ltd
11 Blenheim Court, 316 Woodstock Road, Oxford OX2 7NS, England
www.johnbeaufoy.com

Photo Credits
Front cover: *main image: Arisbe decolor* © Leif Gabrielsen. *Bottom row, left to right: Abisara geza* © Jojo De Peralta, *Cethosia luzonica* © Jade Aster T. Badon, and *Parthenos sylvia* © Jade Aster T. Badon.
Back cover: *Pareronia valeria* © Jade Aster T. Badon
Title page: *Poritia philota* © Leif Gabrielsen
Contents page: *Euploea mulciber* © Jade Aster T. Badon.

Main descriptions Photographs are denoted by a page number followed by t (top), b (bottom), l (left), c (centre) or r (right).

Andrea B. Agillon 82tr, 84br, 88br, 96b, 111bl, 111br, 128tr, 139t. **Shekai Alaban** 40tr, 41b, 59t, 59tbl. **Linda Alisto** 11b, 14br, 19bl, 19br, 20bl, 20br, 23b, 24br, 27bt, 27b, 28b, 34bl, 34br, 36b, 37tl, 37tr, 38tr, 42tl, 42tr, 44tc, 44tr, 45tl, 50tl, 50tr, 53bl, 53br, 54t, 54tb, 54bl, 54br, 56bc, 59rbr, 67t, 73tl, 73tc, 73tr, 74b, 82b, 84bl, 85tl, 85tr, 90t, 94b, 95b, 96tl, 96tr, 98tr, 98b, 102br, 104t, 104bl, 105tl, 107bl, 107br, 108t, 108bl, 108br, 110bl, 110br, 112b, 117t, 117b, 122b, 123tl, 123tr, 123br, 124bl, 124br, 126b, 127t, 128bl, 128br, 130t, 133t, 134bl, 134br, 137b, 142tl, 142tr, 142bl, 142br, 143tl, 149bl, 150b. **Jason Apolonio** 11tl, 11tr, 17br, 19t, 20tl, 20tr, 22t, 27tl, 27tr, 40t, 43bt, 43br, 63tr, 83t. **Jade Aster T. Badon** 24t, 31tl, 31tr, 32bl, 32br, 39bt, 50b, 51bt, 51b, 52t, 57bt, 58tbl, 58tbc, 58tbr, 61bt, 61b, 65b, 72tl, 72tr, 75bl, 76tr, 78t, 79b, 81t, 82tl, 84tl, 88tl, 92tr, 94t, 97bt, 99t, 100bl, 100br, 105tr, 106t, 110t, 116t, 121tl, 121tr, 125b, 132t, 132bl, 132br, 136t, 143tr, 144bl, 144b, 145bl, 147b, 151br. **Noel Buensuceso** 16b. **Cristy Burlace** 15b, 16tl, 16tr, 56bt, 56bl, 56br, 77t, 135b, 150tl. **Jonet Carpio** 59b, 62t, 115t. **Chris and Ana Chafer** 18b, 25t, 26t, 28t, 30 tl, 30tr, 47bl, 47br, 55t, 55tl, 55tr, 58tl, 62bl, 62br, 64t, 64tb, 70b, 76tl, 84tr, 85bl, 86b, 88tr, 92tl, 95tr, 112t, 113t, 120t, 125t, 128tl, 129bl, 129br. **Adrian Constantino** 120b. **Johnny Corcha** 48t. **Jojo De Peralta** 10t, 12t, 12b, 13t, 13bl, 14t, 14bl, 18t, 21b, 29tl, 29b, 32tl, 32tr, 33tl, 33tc, 33bl, 33br, 35t, 35b, 36tl, 36tr, 38b, 39tl, 39tr, 44bl, 44br, 46t, 46bl, 46br, 47tl, 47tr, 48bl, 48br, 49bl, 49br, 51tl, 51tr, 53t, 54bt, 55bl, 55br, 56tl, 56tr, 57tl, 57tc, 57tr, 58bl, 58br, 60tl, 60tr, 60b, 61t, 63b, 64bl, 64br, 65t, 66t, 66tbl, 66tbr, 66b, 67b, 68b, 70t, 71t, 72b, 73b, 74t, 75br, 76b, 77b, 78b, 80br, 81b, 86t, 87t, 87bl, 87br, 88tc, 88bl, 89tl, 89tr, 89b, 90bl, 90br, 92bl, 92br, 93t, 93b, 95tl, 97t, 98tl, 99tl, 99br, 100t, 101t, 101b, 102tl, 106b, 107t, 113b, 114tl, 114tr, 114b, 115b, 116b, 118t, 118b, 119t, 119b, 122t, 124t, 126t, 129tl, 129tr, 130b, 131t, 131bl, 131br, 133b, 134t, 135t, 136b, 137t, 138t, 138b, 140br, 141tl, 141tl, 141b, 143b, 144t, 144bt, 145t, 145bt, 146t, 147t, 148t, 148b, 149t, 149br, 150tr, 151t, 152t. **Romana Delos Reyes** 10b, 22b, 34tr, 43tl, 43tr, 44tl, 83b, 85br, 103tr, 111tl, 140t, 152b. **Leif Gabrielsen** 13br, 15t, 16bt, 25tl, 25br, 26bl, 26br, 30bl, 30bc, 30br, 37bl, 37br, 38tl, 45bl, 45br, 52b, 63rl, 69b, 79t, 91tl, 91tr, 97bl, 97br, 105bl, 109bl, 109br, 123bt, 123bl, 141tl, 146b, 151tl, 153b. **Forest Jarvis** 23t, 68t. **Albert Kang** 57br, 71b, 80t. **Leana Lahom-Cristobal** 17bl, 18bt, 20tc, 21t, 33tr, 34tl, 40bl, 40br, 41tl, 41tr, 45tr, 69t, 75t, 80bl, 103tl, 103br, 104bt, 104br, 105br, 109t, 111tr, 127bl, 139b, 151bl, 153tr. **Jean Henri Oracion** 17t, 24bl, 57bl, 72tc, 140bl. **Fernando Panuculan** 31b. **Gerson Kim Penetrante** 49t. **Veronica Prudente** 58tr. **Harvey Salaga** 102tr. **Tristan Senarillos** 91bl, 91br, 121bl, 121br. **Leni Sutcliffe** 127br. **Agnes Adique Talavera** 29 tr, 40tl, 42bl, 42br, 43bl, 100bt, 102bl, 103bl, 105tc. **Reggie Villahermosa** 39bl, 39br.

Great care has been taken to maintain the accuracy of the information contained in this work. However, neither the publishers nor the authors can be held responsible for any consequences arising from the use of the information contained therein.

ISBN 978-1-913679-05-7

Edited by Krystyna Mayer
Designed by Gulmohur Press, New Delhi
Printed and bound in Malaysia by Times Offset (M) Sdn. Bhd.

·CONTENTS·

INTRODUCTION

The Philippines is an archipelago of more than 7,000 islands, situated in Southeast Asia. The various sizes and ages of the islands resulted in the evolution of unique endemic species of flora and fauna. Currently, the Philippines holds 927 butterfly species, of which a third can only be found in the country. The diversity of butterflies in the Philippines can be attributed to the colonization of related species from neighbouring islands. According to Treadaway & Schroeder (2012), there are five possible routes for neighbouring butterflies to reach the Philippines.

1. Northern route, from mainland Asia to Taiwan and towards north Luzon, through the Batanes and Babuyanes group of islands.
2. From Borneo towards Palawan, through Balabac island.
3. From Borneo to Mindanao, through the Sulu Archipelago and Basilan.
4. From Sulawesi towards the southern part of Mindanao, through the Kepuluan islands.
5. From Halmahera and Talaud islands towards south-east Mindanao.

This book provides information on the identification of butterfly species, the larval foodplants or hosts, and distribution and habitats. The identification is based on observation of the colouration and markings of each butterfly, although some species can have varying forms. The larval foodplants or hosts of most species in the Philippines still need further research, and it is possible that the larvae feed on similar plants to those utilized by butterfly species in other neighbouring countries. The habitats information is based on field observations and literature, and this data may also vary. Depending on how the habitats are changing, some species may alter their local distribution. Species and subspecies distribution information is based on the checklist by Treadaway & Schroeder (2012). Additional locality records documented by citizen scientists, reported to Philippine Lepidoptera Butterflies and Moths, Inc. (PhiLep), are also included.

SPECIES & SUBSPECIES

The islands of the Philippines, of various ages and sizes, saw the evolution of unique species and subspecies, mainly due to isolation. Since the Philippines have several islands and mountain ranges, it is no surprise that several subspecies of a species may occur. Subspecies are organisms that belong to the same species, but due to geographical isolation, on an island or several islands, they are able to maintain consistent forms or characteristics. An example is the Dark Yellow Albatross *Appias nephele*, in which the subspecies in Palawan and Luzon have narrower black markings than the subspecies in the south (Mindanao and the Sulu Archipelago), which have broader black markings.

BUTTERFLY OBSERVATION

The butterflies in the Philippines can be found in various habitats, such as primary and secondary forests, home gardens, open fields, urban areas, and cultivated and agricultural land. Some species can fly at the highest elevations, while others prefer coastal areas. The highest diversity of butterfly species can be found in primary and secondary forests, because some butterflies prefer this type of habitat, and as a result of other factors, such as the presence of their host plants. Here are some tips for observing butterflies in various habitats.

Forests

The forests are the best places to observe butterflies if you are looking for some of the rarest species. Forest trails and edges are the best places to see butterflies in this type of habitat, since some species perch on leaves and sometimes bask on the ground. It is best to walk slowly – careful observation of the surroundings is needed to spot butterflies before they fly away. A camera is helpful, enabling you to capture the charismatic poses of butterflies and their striking colours – information that is useful for further identification later. The best time to observe butterflies in the forests is during sunrise, when their flying activities peak before noon, and also during late afternoons. Butterflies found in forested habitats include those in the genera *Arhopala*, *Cyrestis*, *Ragadia* and *Lexias*.

Cultivated Land

A tract of agricultural land can host several species, depending on the crop that is planted on it, and the chances are that the butterflies seen flying in these areas also feed on the leaves, buds and flowers of the crops. Common butterflies in these areas include *Junonia*, *Mycalesis*, *Hypolimnas* and *Papilio* species.

Urban Areas

Busy towns and cities offer the opportunity to see some butterfly species, and the best places to see them are gardens. Some species, especially those that are distributed throughout the Philippines, fly from island to island, which means that they have to stop somewhere to get nectar. Flowering plants in gardens in urban areas provide nectar not just for local species, but also for migratory ones. Common butterflies in these areas include *Leptosia*, *Catopsilia*, *Zizina* and *Eurema* species.

Coastal Areas

These not only provide excellent beaches, but are also great places to observe the butterfly species inhabiting this habitat. Depending on the island, the vegetation and some flowering plants in coastal areas provide refuge for localized and common butterflies such as *Appias*, *Catopsilia*, *Hasora* and *Jamides* species.

AREAS TO VISIT

If you are planning on observing and photographing butterflies, here are some of the best places in the Philippines for this.

Luzon The island of Luzon hosts several unique species, and some of the areas to visit include the Sierra Madre, which is the country's longest mountain range, Babuyan islands, Batanes and Camiguin de Luzon of Luzon's northernmost islands. Some notable mountainous places include Mt Pulag in Baguio, the mountain ranges of Zambales, the forests of Dona Remedios in the province of Aurora, Mt Palay-Palay National Park in Cavite, Mt Makiling in Laguna and Mt Banahaw in Quezon.

Mindoro There are two mountain peaks in Mindoro, namely Mt Halcon in the northern region and Mt Baco in the south. These two mountains are home to some of the country's endemic species.

Marinduque This island is famous not just for butterflies, but also for its annual butterfly festival.

Palawan Due to this region's geological history, its butterflies are similar to the ones found in Borneo and Malaysia, which is why Palawan hosts several unique species. You will never miss the butterflies when hiking towards the peak of Cleopatra's Needle.

Panay The mountain ranges, especially Mt Madja-as, on the western side of the island, are home to some of the country's endemic species.

Negros The best areas to observe butterflies on this island are Mt Talinis and Balinsasayao Twin Lakes Natural Park, the forest of Mt Canlaon and North Negros Natural Park.

Samar Samar Island Natural Park and the other remaining forests on the island are home to the Philippines' eastern endemic butterflies.

Leyte Situated in the middle of Samar to the north and Mindanao to the south, Leyte island is known as one of the islands that have frequently been visited by butterfly experts and enthusiasts.

Cebu The remaining forests and ravines of Cebu island still hold a great diversity of the Philippines' butterflies, and a visit to the Julian Jumalon's Butterfly Sanctuary is a must.

Bohol The hills of Bohol offer not just a great sight but also the unique butterflies on this island. The best place to see various species is the Habitat Bohol Butterfly Garden in Bilar.

Siquijor The best way to see butterflies on this small island is to visit or drive by the Bulalakaw Forests Reserve and Bandilaan Natural Park.

Mindanao The vast lands and mountainous regions of Mindanao paved the way for butterflies to diversify into several endemic species. Some notable areas for butterflies include Mt Malindang, Mt Apo, Mt Kitanglad, Mt Hamiguitan, Mt Tagubud and Mt Busa.

Some Butterfly Facts

Butterflies (and moths) belong to a huge order of insects, known as the Lepidoptera, which has more than 165,000 species worldwide. Most feed on nectar and other liquids, probing flowers with a long, slender tongue (proboscis). The larvae (or caterpillars) feed on plants, though a small number also feed on ant grubs.

The Life Cycle

As is the case with all insects, butterflies' life cycles include a number of stages. The first stage is the egg, which is generally laid by the female on the plant on which the caterpillar (larva) will feed. The caterpillar hatches from the egg. Butterfly larvae look nothing like the adult insect, being worm-like in appearance, with some having spectacular patterning and forms. A caterpillar moults several times, then metamorphoses into the chrysalis, or pupa. This has a hard outer skin and hardly moves at all. Inside, its tissues liquefy and it develops into the adult insect.

Mimicry

There are some instances – termed mimicry – when certain butterflies of different species can look very similar. This occurs in order to increase a butterfly species' chances of survival. As an example, the female Danaid Eggfly *Hypolimnas misippus* mimics the Plain Tiger *Danaus chrysippus*. The caterpillar of the latter feeds on some plants that contain toxins, then accumulates the toxins in its body; due to the presence of the toxins, predators avoid eating it. Thus butterfly species that mimic this butterfly increase their chance of survival by being avoided by predators.

Identification & Taxonomy

As already mentioned, this book follows the checklist of Treadaway & Schroeder (2012), with some changes published by various authors. Some of the butterfly species – especially the endemics of the Philippines – do not have common names, and PhiLep are currently proposing names for them.

The easiest way to identify a butterfly is through its family first, then the genus. When local guides or amateur researchers spot a butterfly, they first identify which family it belongs to by its size (the wingspan is given after the scientific name in the descriptions that follow) and colouration, then identify its genus based on the characteristics that are unique to that specific genus. As an example, first of all the Scarlet Mormon *Menelaides deiphobus* is large, so it belongs to the family Papilionidae; then it can be identified as a large black butterfly with red markings on the wings. This information provides preliminary identification of the butterfly as the Scarlet Mormon.

With advancements in genetic studies, it is not surprising that species are constantly being revised, with some placed in new genera, and others elevated to species or demoted to subspecies.

Wing Parts

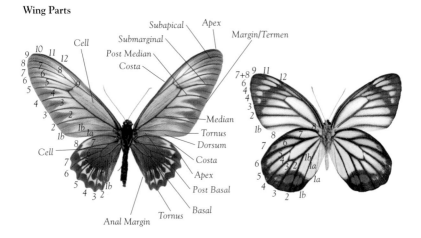

GLOSSARY

abdomen Rear segment of body, behind thorax.

anal region Wing region close to anus or abdomen.

antenna (pl. **antennae**) Pair of sensory organs on an insect's head.

anterior Front of body.

apex Frontal corner of wing.

aposematic Refers to conspicuous pattern or bright colouration of an organism, warning predators of its toxicity or unpalatable taste.

caudal At or near back half of body

cell Middle part of wing (rectangular or oblong shaped), where most wing veins are connected.

costa Leading edge of wing, perpendicular to body.

cremaster Hook-like bottom tip of pupa.

cryptic Camouflaged by body colour and/or shape.

diapause Period of suspended development.

dimorphism Distinct physical differences between sexes.

distal Section of limb or attachment furthest from body.

diurnal Active during the day.

dorsal Upper surface, or back.

endemic Found only in a certain area.

family Taxonomic rank above genus and below order.

femur Section of leg close to body, attached to tibia. The short trochanter and coxa sections attach it to the body.

foodplant Plant that a caterpillar (or larva) feeds on.

forewing Anterior (front) wing.

genus (pl. **genera**) Taxonomic group above species and below family.

girdle Silk thread used to support pupa.

gregarious Living within a group or community.

herbivorous Feeding only on plant matter.

hindwing Posterior (back) wing.

invertebrate Animal that lacks backbone.

larva (pl. **larvae**) Newly hatched, wingless stage of an animal. The caterpillar in butterflies.

mandibles Jaw-like mouthparts used for grasping and cutting.

margin Edge of wing parallel to body.

median Refers to middle section or region of wing.

mimicry When a species mimics/copies physical appearance of another species.

nectarivorous Refers to animals that feed purely on nectar.

nocturnal Active at night.

order Taxonomic rank above family and below class.

osmeterium Fleshy, scent-producing gland used for defence. Found in Papilionidae caterpillars.

ovipositor Specialized organ on abdomen of some female insects. Used for depositing eggs into plant material, animals or egg chambers.

parasite Organism that lives on or within another for its own benefit (for example for food or shelter).

posterior Back of body.

proboscis Long, mobile feeding tube extending from front of head, seen in insects.

prothorax Segment of thorax near head.

pupation Development into pupa.

seta (pl. **setae**) Stiff structure resembling a hair.

species Basic unit of taxonomic classification.

subapex Refers to region just below apex of wing.

submargin Refers to region just below margin of wing.

subspecies Level of taxonomic division below species.

substrate Underlying layer or material on which an organism lives.

tarsus (pl. **tarsi**) Final section of an insect's leg, attached to tibia, often divided into segments called tarsomeres.

taxonomy Classification of living things based on characteristics.

terrestrial Living on or spending time on the ground.

territory Area that an individual or group occupies and protects.

thorax Middle section of body of insect, between head and abdomen.

tibia Distal section of insect's leg between femur and tarsus.

tornus (tornal region) Posterior edge of wing.

tubercle Raised projection.

ventral Undersurface or belly of an animal.

BIRDWINGS & SWALLOWTAILS

White Dragontail
■ *Lamproptera curius* 19mm

DESCRIPTION Small butterfly with long tails and white median bands on both wings. **LARVAL FOODPLANTS** *Illigera* species (Hernandiaceae family). **DISTRIBUTION** Subspecies *curius* occurs in Balabac and Palawan. **HABITATS** Mostly found mud-puddling on riversides and lake shores, in forested habitats.

Tailed Jay ■ *Graphium agamemnon* 45–49mm

DESCRIPTION Medium-sized butterfly with green and black wing markings. Flies swiftly. **LARVAL FOODPLANTS** Various plants such as *Cinnamomum* (Lauraceae), *Magnolia* and *Michelia* (Magnoliaceae), *Artabotrys, Annona, Desmos, Friesodielsia, Mitrephora, Polyalthia, Saccopetalum* and *Uvaria* (Annonaceae). **DISTRIBUTION** Found throughout the Philippines. **HABITATS** Common butterfly that flies in various habitats, and can be seen flying swiftly in home gardens.

Common Bluebottle ■ *Graphium sarpedon* 43–36mm

DESCRIPTION Medium-sized butterfly with black and bluish-greenish bands on both wings. **LARVAL FOODPLANTS** *Cinnamomum, Crytocarya, Endiandra, Neolitsea* and *Litsea* (Lauraceae), *Geijera* (Rutaceae), *Tristania* (Myrtaceae), *Planchonella* (Sapindaceae), *Daphnandra* and *Doryphora* (Atherospermataceae), and *Macaranga* (Euphorbiaceae). **DISTRIBUTION** Found throughout the Philippines. **HABITATS** Common butterfly that flies swiftly in various habitats, but commonly encountered in forested areas.

Common Jay ■ *Arisbe doson* 35mm

DESCRIPTION Medium-sized butterfly similar to other *Arisbe* and *Graphium* species. Distinguished from them by basal red spot with black markings not fused with black band of anal margin. **LARVAL FOODPLANTS** Various plants such as *Magnolia, Michelia, Rauwenhoffia, Uvaria, Annona, Desmos, Polyalthia, Diploglottis, Cinnamomum* and *Mithrephora*. **DISTRIBUTION** Subspecies *gyndes* occurs in western islands such as Palawan, Dumaran and Calamian; subspecies *evemonides* in Balabac, Bongao, Mapun, Sanga Sanga, Sibutu and Tawi Tawi; subspecies *nauta* in Basilan, Bohol, Catanduanes, Cebu, Dinagat, Homonhon, Jolo, Leyte, Lubang, Luzon, Marinduque, Masbate, Mindoro, Mindanao, Negros, Panaon, Pollilo, Samar, Siargao, Sibuyan, Siquijor, Tablas and Ticao; subspecies *postianus* in Batanes. **HABITATS** Same flight pattern as the other species. Found in various habitats, including forests and home gardens.

Spotted Jay
■ *Arisbe arycles* 32mm

DESCRIPTION
Greenish markings on
wings highly outlined
with black. Conspicuous
red markings on
hindwings. **LARVAL
FOODPLANTS** Not
known, but probably
similar to those for
other *Arisbe* species.
DISTRIBUTION
Subspecies *perinthus*
occurs in Palawan,
Calamian and Balabac.
HABITATS Flies in
lowland areas and can be
seen at forest edges.

Veined Jay
■ *Arisbe bathycles*
34–40mm

DESCRIPTION
Looks similar to
Spotted Jay (above),
but is bluish with
yellow markings
near base of
hindwing. **LARVAL
FOODPLANTS** Not
known, but probably
same as those for
other *Arisbe* species.
DISTRIBUTION
Subspecies *bathycloides*
occurs in Palawan,
Calamian and
Balabac. **HABITATS**
Flies along forest
edges, similarly to
Spotted.

Chain Swordtail

■ *Arisbe aristeus* 30–40mm

DESCRIPTION Medium-sized butterfly with black and creamy-white markings on both wings, and conspicuous red marks on mid-section of hindwing. Long hindwing tails. **LARVAL FOODPLANTS** *Mitrephora* and *Polyalthia*; species from Leguminosae family also recorded. **DISTRIBUTION** Subspecies *hermocrates* occurs throughout the Philippines. **HABITATS** Found in various habitats.

Swordtail Jay ■ *Arisbe decolor* 39mm

DESCRIPTION Similar to Chain Swordtail (above) but greener, with triangular or broad, pointy black markings. Yellow-orange markings near margin of hindwing. **LARVAL FOODPLANTS** Not known, but probably the same as for other *Arisbe* species. **DISTRIBUTION** Subspecies *neozebraica* occurs in Luzon, Bohol, Leyte, Marinduque, Masbate, Negros, Panay, Panaon, Polillo, Samar, Siquijor and Ticao; subspecies *decolor* in Balabac, Calamian and Palawan; subspecies *atratus* in Mindoro; subspecies *sibuyana* in Sibuyan; subspecies *tigris* in Dinagat and Mindanao; subspecies *rebeccae* in Camiguin de Luzon (Babuyanes islands); subspecies *jamesi* in Sibutu and Sanga Sanga. **HABITATS** Flies swiftly and found in various habitats.

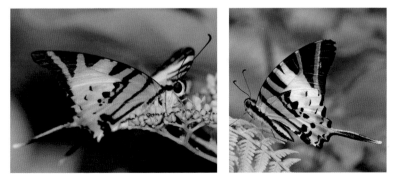

Lesser Zebra

■ *Arisbe macareus* 45mm

DESCRIPTION Medium-sized butterfly with broader and wider wings compared to other *Arisbe* species. Black with broad white band markings on both wings, and white spots on wing margins. **LARVAL FOODPLANTS** Not known, but probably the same as for other *Arisbe* species. **DISTRIBUTION** Subspecies *palawanicola* occurs in Balabac and Palawan, with one record from Mindoro. **HABITATS** Flies in forested habitats and can be seen puddling with other *Arisbe*.

Palawan Birdwing ■ *Trogonoptera trojana* 86–96mm

DESCRIPTION Large butterfly with narrow forewings and reddish body. Generally black with triangular or leaf-like metallic markings near margins of both wings. Underside has metallic blue markings. Female dark brown with blue, green and white pointy markings. **LARVAL FOODPLANTS** *Aristolochia foveolata* (Aristolochiaceae family). **DISTRIBUTION** Occurs in Palawan and possibly in Balabac. **HABITATS** Flies in forested habitats and may wander into nearby gardens. Males tend to fly at ground level while most females fly around tree-tops.

LEFT Female; RIGHT Male

Golden Birdwing ■ *Troides rhadamantus* 64–79mm

DESCRIPTION Large black butterfly with metallic golden markings on hindwings. Female larger than male, with broader black and golden markings on hindwings. **LARVAL FOODPLANTS** *Aristolochia tagala* (Aristolochiaceae family). **DISTRIBUTION** Subspecies *rhadamantus* found throughout the Philippines, except in some of western islands such as Balabac, Calamian, Dumaran and Palawan, where subspecies *plateni* occurs. **HABITATS** Prefers to fly near shaded areas and occasionally visits gardens to sip nectar.

Pink Rose ■ *Pachliopta kotzebuea* 45mm

DESCRIPTION Medium-sized black butterfly with pinkish/reddish, crescent-shaped markings near margins of hindwings. **LARVAL FOODPLANTS** *Aristolochia* (Aristolochiaceae family). **DISTRIBUTION** Subspecies *philippus* occurs in Camiguin de Mindanao, Dinagat, Homonhon, Leyte, Mindanao, Panaon, Samar, Sarangani and Siargao; subspecies *kotzebuea* in central to west Luzon; subspecies *bilara* in Bohol and Cebu; subspecies *deseileus* in Marinduque, Masbate, Mindoro, Negros, Panay, Sibuyan and Ticao; subspecies *mataconga* in south Luzon; subspecies *tindongana* in Babuyan and north-east Luzon; subspecies *calataganensis* in Catanduanes. **HABITATS** Flies in various habitats, such as home gardens and forest edges.

Batwing ■ *Atrophaneura semperi* 69–78mm

DESCRIPTION Large black butterfly with reddish body and some red or pink markings on hindwings. Variable, and males can be identified by their semi-folded hindwings. **LARVAL FOODPLANTS** *Aristolochia* (Aristolochiaceae family). **DISTRIBUTION** Subspecies *supernotatus* occurs in Bohol, Cebu, Camiguin de Mindanao, Leyte, Panaon and Samar; subspecies *semperi* in Camiguin de Luzon, extreme south-east of Luzon and Pollilo; subspecies *albofasciata* in Mindoro; subspecies *aphthonia* in Dinagat, Mindanao and Siargao; subspecies *baglantis* in Negros; subspecies *imogene* in Sibuyan; subspecies *lizae* in Panay; subspecies *melanotus* in Calamian and Palawan; subspecies *sorsogona* in extreme south-east of Luzon; subspecies *justini* in Masbate. **HABITATS** Flies in forested habitats, and can be seen nectaring in nearby home gardens and forest edges. In Negros, known to fly with Golden Birdwing (p. 15).

LEFT *Female; RIGHT Male*

Common Mime
■ *Chilasa clytia* 52mm

DESCRIPTION Large, dark brown butterfly with three conspicuous short white bands on apex of forewings. Hindwings have arrow-shaped markings near margins. **LARVAL FOODPLANTS** *Litsea* and *Cinnamomum* (Lauraceae family). **DISTRIBUTION** Subspecies *visayensis* occurs in Bohol, Cebu, Leyte, Negros, Panay, Samar and Siquijor; subspecies *palephates* in Catanduanes, Luzon, Marinduque and Mindoro; subspecies *duboisi* in Babuyan; subspecies *panopinus* in Balabac, Busuanga, Cuyo, Dumaran and Palawan; subspecies *anuus* in Sibuyan; subspecies *gulam* in Basilan and Mindanao; subspecies *partidu* in Jolo. **HABITATS** Common butterfly that flies in various habitats, including on mountain peaks.

Emerald Peacock Swallowtail ■ *Achillides palinurus* 56–59mm

DESCRIPTION Large butterfly with conspicuous metallic green median bands on both wings. Flashes metallic colouration when flying during sunny days. **LARVAL FOODPLANTS** *Clausena* and *Toddalia* (Rutaceae family). **DISTRIBUTION** Subspecies *daedalus* occurs in almost all the islands, while subspecies *angustatus* is found in western islands such as Palawan, Cuyo, Dumaran, Busuanga and Balabac. **HABITATS** Common butterfly that flies swiftly at canopy level in forested areas, and occasionally visits gardens for nectar.

Common Lime Butterfly ■ *Papilio demoleus* 48–50mm

DESCRIPTION Medium-sized butterfly distinguishable by 'leopard' pattern on both wings. **LARVAL FOODPLANTS** *Citrus* and *Atalantia*. Mostly Rutaceae family. **DISTRIBUTION** Subspecies *demoleus* occurs throughout the Philippines. **HABITATS** Common and abundant butterfly that flies in various habitats.

Banded Swallowtail

■ *Papilio demolion* 48–54mm

DESCRIPTION Large butterfly with narrow black forewings and yellow circular patches that form narrow yellow band on forewing. Hindwings have arrow-shaped yellow markings near margins. **LARVAL FOODPLANTS** *Luvunga scandens* and other citrus plants. **DISTRIBUTION** Subspecies *delostenus* occurs in Palawan. **HABITATS** Flies in forested habitats, and can be seen puddling on nearby lakes and rivers.

Scarlet Mormon ■ *Menelaides deiphobus* 76–78mm

DESCRIPTION Large black butterfly with powdery white on upperside of hindwings and red markings on underside. Female variable, with white, red or yellow markings on wings. **LARVAL FOODPLANTS** *Citrus* plants. **DISTRIBUTION** Subspecies *rumanzovia* found almost throughout the Philippines, except Palawan down to islands of Tawitawi, where subspecies *tarawakana* occurs. **HABITATS** Common garden and forest butterfly that prefers to fly near or under shaded areas.

Common Mormon ■ *Menelaides polytes* 50mm

DESCRIPTION Medium-sized butterfly smaller than Scarlet Mormom (opposite). Male black with yellow-white spots on margins of forewings, larger and forming band on

hindwings. Female variable, but commonly has large white and red-orange patch on middle section of hindwing. Another female form looks exactly like male. **LARVAL FOODPLANTS** Various plants such as *Citrus*, *Fortunella*, *Glycosmis*, *Zanthoxylum*, *Toddalia*, *Murraya*, *Triphasia*, *Aegle*, *Euodia*, *Clausena*, *Alatantia* and *Poncirus*. **DISTRIBUTION** Subspecies *ledebouria* occurs throughout the Philippines, except in Batanes (subspecies *pasikrates*); subspecies *steffi* in Bongao, Sanga Sanga, Sibutu and Tawi Tawi. **HABITATS** Common garden and forest butterfly.

Red Helen ■ *Menelaides helenus* 50–75mm

DESCRIPTION Large black butterfly with four conspicuous yellow-white bands (of various sizes) on hindwing. **LARVAL FOODPLANTS** *Citrus*, *Toddalia* and *Zanthoxylum*. **DISTRIBUTION** Subspecies *hystaspes* occurs in almost all islands, except Palawan, Bongao, Balabac, Sanga Sanga, Sibutu and Tawi Tawi; subspecies *palawanicus* in Palawan and Balabac; subspecies *boloboca* in Sanga Sanga and Tawi Tawi. **HABITATS** Flies swiftly at canopy level, and occasionally visits gardens for nectar.

WHITES, YELLOWS, ORANGE TIPS & SULPHURS

Mottled Emigrant ■ *Catopsilia pyranthe* 36mm

DESCRIPTION Pale green, medium-sized butterfly with black markings (broader in females) on apex of forewings. **LARVAL FOODPLANTS** *Cassia* plants. **DISTRIBUTION** Subspecies *pyranthe* occurs throughout the Philippines. **HABITATS** Common and abundant butterfly that flies in various habitats.

Common Emigrant ■ *Catopsilia pomona* 35mm

DESCRIPTION Medium-sized butterfly that looks like Mottled Emigrant (above), but this species is pale green with yellowish composition on both wings. Female variable, with form that is completely yellow and has more pronounced black markings. **LARVAL FOODPLANTS** *Cassia*, *Senna*, *Butea* and *Bauhinia*. **DISTRIBUTION** Subspecies *pomona* occurs throughout the Philippines. **HABITATS** Common and abundant butterfly that flies in various habitats, and flies with both Mottled Emigrant and Orange Emigrant (opposite).

Orange Emigrant ▪ *Catopsilia scylla* 33mm

DESCRIPTION Medium-sized butterfly with white forewings and yellow hindwings. Male has black marking on costa and apex of forewing. Female variable, and can have broader black markings on both wings. **LARVAL FOODPLANTS** *Cassia* plants. **DISTRIBUTION** Subspecies *cornelia* occurs in Balabac, Bongao, Calamian, Catanduanes, Luzon, Mapun, Marinduque, Mindoro, Palawan, Sanga Sanga, Sibutu and Tawi Tawi; subspecies *asema* in Basilan, Bohol, Cebu, Camiguin de Mindanao, Dinagat, Guimaras, Leyte, Masbate, Mindanao, Negros, Panay, Panaon and Samar. **HABITATS** Common and abundant butterfly, which flies with other *Catopsilia*.

Tree Yellow ▪ *Gandaca harina* 23–25mm

DESCRIPTION Small to medium-sized yellow butterfly with conspicuous black markings on apices; narrower on margins of forewings. Underside pure yellow without black or brown markings. Female similar to male, but paler. **LARVAL FOODPLANTS** *Ventilago* plants (Rhamnaceae family). **DISTRIBUTION** Subspecies *palawanica* occurs in Balabac, Calamian and Palawan; subspecies *mindanaensis* throughout the Philippines, except islands of Balabac, Basilan, Calamian, Palawan and Sulu; subspecies *elis* in Bongao, Jolo, Sanga Sanga, Sibutu and Tawi Tawi; subspecies *gardineri* in Basilan. **HABITATS** Found in forested areas and seen puddling on nearby riverbanks and lakeshores with *Eurema* species.

Common Grass Yellow ▪ *Eurema hecabe* 21mm

DESCRIPTION Small, black and yellow butterfly. Black marking on forewing curves into right angle at vein 4. Underside cell of forewing has two spots (sometimes absent). Female relatively paler than male, with broader black markings on margins of wings. Underside apical black patch on forewing may be absent. **LARVAL FOODPLANTS** *Aeschynomene*,

Cassia, *Leucaena* and *Sesbania*. **DISTRIBUTION** Subspecies *tamiathis* occurs throughout the Philippines, excluding islands of Babuyan, Balabac, Calamian, Lubang, Luzon, Mindoro, Palawan and Sulu. Subspecies *sintica* only found in Mindoro island; subspecies *hecabe* in Babuyan, Balabac, Calamian, Jolo, Lubang, Luzon, Palawan, Sanga Sanga, Siasi and Tawi Tawi. **HABITATS** Common butterfly that flies in home gardens, cities and disturbed habitats. Also along roadsides and forest edges.

Three-spot Grass Yellow ▪ *Eurema blanda* 23mm

DESCRIPTION Small, black and yellow butterfly that looks similar to Common Grass Yellow (above), but forewings are longer and narrower. Name recalls underside cell of

forewing, which has three spots. Some variations can have very broad black markings. **LARVAL FOODPLANTS** Plants in Fabaceae family, similarly to Common. **DISTRIBUTION** Subspecies *vallivolans* occurs in Basilan, Bohol, Bongao, Calamian, Cebu, Dinagat, Leyte, Mapun, Mindanao, Negros, Palawan, Panaon, Samar, Sarangani, Sibutu and Tawi Tawi; subspecies *visellia* in Luzon and Mindoro. **HABITATS** Flies in various disturbed habitats with both Common Grass Yellow and Scalloped Grass Yellow *E. laeta*.

Changeable Grass Yellow ■ *Eurema simulatrix* 25mm

DESCRIPTION Small, yellow and black butterfly with long, irregular black ('zigzag') markings on cell of forewing underside. Black marginal marking on hindwing upperside wavy or forms curvy pattern.
LARVAL FOODPLANTS Probably plants similar to those for other *Eurema* species.
DISTRIBUTION Subspecies *simulatrix* occurs in Bohol, Leyte, Mindanao, Negros, Panaon and Samar; subspecies *princesae* in Palawan and Balabac.
HABITATS Mostly documented in forested habitats; rarely flies in disturbed habitats.

Chocolate Grass Yellow ■ *Eurema sarilata* 21–25mm

DESCRIPTION Black and yellow butterfly that is smaller than other *Eurema* species. This species distinguishable by 'chocolate bar' marking on underside apex of forewing.
LARVAL FOODPLANTS *Wallaceodendron* (Fabaceae) and *Ventilago* (Rhamnaceae).

DISTRIBUTION Subspecies *risa* occurs in Cebu, Masbate, Negros, Panay and Siquijor; subspecies *aquilo* in Luzon and Marinduque; subspecies *sarilata* in Dinagat, Leyte, Mindanao, Panaon and Samar; subspecies *boholensis* in Bohol; subspecies *dayani* in Bongao, Sanga Sanga, Sibutu and Tawi Tawi; subspecies *mindorana* in Mindoro; subspecies *perplexa* in Basilan; subspecies *rosario* in Homonhon; subspecies *sibuyanensis* in Sibuyan.
HABITATS Flies in forested habitats and can be seen along forest trails.

Yellow Jezebel ▪ *Delias themis* 35mm

DESCRIPTION Medium-sized butterfly with white wings (with pale yellow composition on hindwings), and black markings on forewing apices and marginal region of hindwings. Underside of forewing white with black markings on apical region. Hindwing yellow with single yellow spot and white spots on submarginal region. **LARVAL FOODPLANTS** Currently unknown, but probably *Loranthus* (Loranthaceae family). **DISTRIBUTION** Subspecies *soteira* occurs in Luzon, Marinduque and Polillo; subspecies *mihoae* in Negros Island; subspecies *kawamurai* in Mindoro; subspecies *themis* in Bohol, Cebu, Camiguin de Mindanao, Leyte, Mindanao, Panaon and Samar; subspecies *yuii* in Masbate and Panay. **HABITATS** Mostly found in forested habitats.

Painted Jezebel ▪ *Delias hyparete* 38mm

DESCRIPTION Medium-sized butterfly. Hindwing underside has submarginal, medium to large red spots, except on spaces 7 and 8. In some races, some red spots absent. Hindwing has contrasting yellow and white colouration. Female has broader black markings than male. **LARVAL FOODPLANTS** *Loranthus* (Loranthaceae family), commonly called mistletoe. **DISTRIBUTION** Subspecies *luzonensis* occurs in Bohol, Cebu, Camiguin de Luzon, Camiguin de Mindanao, Dinagat, Leyte, Lubang, Luzon, Marinduque, Mindoro, north-east Mindanao, Negros, Panay, Panaon, Pollilo, Samar and Sibuyan; subspecies *palawanica* in Calamian and Palawan; subspecies *domorana* in Dumaran; subspecies *lucina* in Jolo; subspecies *noellindae* in Basilan; subspecies *melville* in Balabac; subspecies *mindanaensis* in Mindanao, excluding north-east Mindanao. **HABITATS** Flies in various habitats, including home gardens, but mostly abundant in forested habitats.

Common Jezebel ■ *Delias henningia* 34–40mm

DESCRIPTION Medium-sized butterfly. Upperside black with median white band and yellow markings on hindwings. Underside black with narrow, pointy white markings on apical region of forewing, and conspicuous white median band. Hindwing has red basal markings and small to large yellow bands. **LARVAL FOODPLANTS** *Loranthus* (Loranthaceae) and Euphorbia (Euphorbiaceae). **DISTRIBUTION** Subspecies *henningia* occurs in Biliran, Catanduanes, Cebu, Caminguin de Mindanao, Leyte, Lubang, Luzon, Marinduque, Masbate, Mindoro, Negros, Panay, Panaon and Samar; subspecies *camotana* in Camotes island; subspecies *ochreopicta* in Basilan and Mindanao; subspecies *romblonensis* in Sibuyan and Romblon; subspecies *pandemia* in Palawan, Calamian and Balabac; subspecies *voconia* in Bohol. **HABITATS** Flies in various habitats with Painted Jezebel (opposite), but commonly encountered in forested habitats.

Black Jezebel ■ *Delias diaphana* 45mm

DESCRIPTION Large butterfly. Male has white-bluish with black markings on apices to subapices of forewings. Underside almost black, with white markings throughout wings. In female, upperside black with yellow markings on forewings, and white patch on hindwing. Underside looks similar to male's, but has more yellow markings, especially on forewing cell. **LARVAL FOODPLANTS** Currently unknown, but probably *Loranthus* species. **DISTRIBUTION** Subspecies *diaphana* occurs in north-south-central Mindanao; subspecies *sakagutti* in east-south-east Mindanao; subspecies *basilisae* in north-west Mindanao (Mt Malindang); subspecies *yatai* in north-east Mindanao (Mt Tandag); subspecies *treadawayi* in Panay island. **HABITATS** Mostly flies in forested habitats; may fly towards nearby home gardens.

Psyche ▪ *Leptosia nina* 18–28mm

DESCRIPTION Small, dirty-white butterfly with conspicuous black spot on apex and subapex of forewing. **LARVAL FOODPLANTS** *Cleome* (Cleomaceae) and *Crateva* (Capparaceae). **DISTRIBUTION** Subspecies *terentia* occurs in Basilan, Bohol, Calamian, Cebu, Cuyo, Dinagat, Mindoro, Mindanao, Negros, Palawan, Panay, Samar and Sarangani; subspecies *asukae* in Jolo; subspecies *georgi* in Luzon; subspecies *malayana* in Sanga Sanga, Sibutu and Tawi Tawi. **HABITATS** Common and abundant in lowland areas. Prefers to fly weakly near ground level on grassy areas and along roadsides.

Orange Gull ▪ *Cepora aspasia* 31mm

DESCRIPTION Medium-sized butterfly. Upperside forewing white with broad black lines on veins. Hindwing yellow with broad black margins. Underside similar to upperside, but with yellow-white apical spots on forewings. Female has broader dark brown submargins on hindwing than male, and subspecies *olgina* is dark to pale brown. **LARVAL FOODPLANTS** *Capparis* (Capparidaceae family). **DISTRIBUTION** Subspecies *tolmida* occurs in Cebu and Camotes; subspecies *orantia* in Bohol, Leyte, Mindanao and Samar; subspecies *olga* in Babuyan, Batanes, Luzon (excluding north-west region) and Marinduque; subspecies *olgina* in Palawan and Calamian; subspecies *anaitis* in north-west Luzon; subspecies *fulcinea* in Polillo; subspecies *irma* in Bongao, Jolo, Sanga Sanga, Siasi, Sibutu and Tawi Tawi; subspecies *phokaia* in Balabac; subspecies *poetelia* in Camiguin de Mindanao; subspecies *rhemia* in Lubang, Masbate, Mindoro, Negros, Panay, Sibuyan and Siquijor; subspecies *zisca* in Basilan. **HABITATS** Flies in various habitats, and can be seen flying swiftly along forest edges.

Eastern Striped Albatross ▪ *Appias olferna* 27–28mm

DESCRIPTION Medium-sized white butterfly with pointy black and white markings on margins of wings (male). Female similar but darker on upperside, with forewing median band. Undersides of both sexes similar, but female's has more black and yellow composition. **LARVAL FOODPLANTS** Capparidaceae such as *Crateva* and *Capparis* (Capparidaceae), and *Cleome* (Cleomaceae family). **DISTRIBUTION** Subspecies *peducaea* found in Bohol,

Cebu, Caminguin de Mindanao, Jolo, Luzon, Marinduque, Mindoro, Mindanao, Negros and Palawan. **HABITATS** Common butterfly that flies swiftly in various habitats.

LEFT Female; RIGHT Male

Chocolate Albatross
▪ *Appias lyncida* 35mm

DESCRIPTION Medium-sized butterfly. Male white with pointy black markings on margins of both wings. Forewing underside white with black wing margins, and yellow or white spot on subapical region. Hindwing underside yellow with black margins. Female upperside dark brown to almost black, with narrow, pointy white markings. Underside of female black; white markings on forewing; hindwing black (on margins), white and yellow. **LARVAL FOODPLANTS** Capparidaceae such as *Crateva* and *Capparis*. **DISTRIBUTION** Subspecies *enaretina* occurs in Balabac, Palawan and Calamian; subspecies *lepidana* in Guimaras, Masbate, Negros, Panay, Romblon and Sibuyan; subspecies *andrea* in Lubang, Luzon, Marinduque, Mindoro and Mindanao; subspecies *maccina* in Cuyo and Dumaran; subspecies *subenarete* in Bongao, Sanga Sanga and Tawi Tawi. **HABITATS** Flies in various habitats, but commonly found in lowland areas, especially in home gardens.

TOP Female; ABOVE Male

Orange Albatross ▪ *Appias nero* 30–35mm

DESCRIPTION Medium-sized butterfly. Male orange or dark orange with black wing margins. Underside similar but paler. Female variable – orange or white and with pale or broad black margins on both wings. Orange or white markings on submarginal region of both wings, absent in some subspecies. **LARVAL FOODPLANTS** *Capparis* (Capparidaceae family). **DISTRIBUTION** Subspecies *palawanica* occurs in Balabac and Palawan; subspecies *corazonae* in Bongao, Sanga Sanga and Sibutu; subspecies *domitia* in Babuyan, Batanes, Luzon and Marinduque; subspecies *fleminius* in Mindoro; subspecies *soranus* in Cebu, Masbate, Negros, Panay and Sibuyan; subspecies *tibericus* in Basilan; subspecies *zamboanga* in Bohol, Dinagat, Leyte, Mindanao, Panaon and Samar; subspecies *flavius* in Turtle islands. **HABITATS** Flies mostly in forested habitats and may visit nearby gardens. Has been noted to mud-puddle with other species in this family.

Banded Puffin ▪ *Appias phoebe* 30–33mm

DESCRIPTION Medium-sized butterfly that flies at higher elevations (above 1,500m). Upperside varies from white to pale yellow, with forewing black apical to marginal markings, and 2–3 white spots on submarginal. Conspicuous black spot on cell end of forewing. Underside looks similar but has purplish composition, and black marking on forewing much reduced to arching black band. Female has broader black markings than male. **LARVAL FOODPLANTS** No information, but probably high-elevation plant species similar to those for other *Appias* species. **DISTRIBUTION** Subspecies *montana* occurs in northern Negros (Mt Kanlaon); subspecies *phoebe* in south and north Luzon; subspecies *mindana* in north-west Mindanao; subspecies *rowelli* in south Palawan; subspecies *zamorra* in Mindoro; subspecies *nuydai* in south Negros (Mt Talinis). **HABITATS** Only found at higher elevations. Can be spotted at forest edges and may also be seen puddling on lakeshores.

Common Albatross ◾ *Appias albina* 30mm

DESCRIPTION Medium-sized butterfly. Male white with pointy apex of forewing. Female can be white or pale orange, with black wing margins. In female, two large white spots (others are tiny) on subapical region of forweing. Undersides of both sexes silvery-white, and females can have white or orange markings and black (with purple composition), curving band on subapical of forewing. **LARVAL FOODPLANTS** *Drypetes* (Euphorbiaceae family). **DISTRIBUTION** Subspecies *semperi* occurs in Babuyan, Bohol, Calamian, Cebu, Guimaras, Lubang, Luzon, Marinduque, Mindoro and Negros; subspecies *pancheia* in Dumaran, Mindanao and Palawan; subspecies *albina* in Balabac, Bongao, Mapun, Sanga Sanga, Sibutu and Tawi Tawi. **HABITATS** Flies in various habitats, including forests and lowland home gardens.

LEFT Male; RIGHT Female

Forest White ◾ *Appias aegis* 23–25mm

DESCRIPTION Small to medium-sized white butterfly with curving black marking on upperside of forewings, with 2–3 pointy protrusions. Underside white with paler black markings on apical region of forewing. Female has broader black markings than male, which occupy most of wings, and conspicuous zigzag median white band on forewing. Underside has similar characteristics, but with dark yellow to orange composition. **LARVAL FOODPLANTS** Probably plants in Capparidaceae family. **DISTRIBUTION** Subspecies *illana* occurs in Babuyan, Biliran, Bohol, Luzon, Cebu, Negros, Mindoro and Marinduque; subspecies *caepia* in Palawan; subspecies *aegis* in Leyte, Mindanao and Samar; subspecies *sibutana* in Sibutu. **HABITATS** Flies in forested habitats, and can also be seen puddling near rivers and nearby areas with flowering plants.

Malaysian Albatross ■ *Saletera panda* 27–30mm

DESCRIPTION Medium-sized butterfly. Male has triangular forewings with upperside creamy-white with black wing margins, and yellow underside. Female has rounder wings, with broad black wing margins; underside yellow with purplish scaling and black band curving from costa to subapical region, and towards tornus of forewing. **LARVAL FOODPLANTS** Currently unknown. **DISTRIBUTION** Subspecies *nathalia* occurs in Luzon, Marinduque, Masbate, Mindoro, Negros, Panay and Polillo; subspecies *distanti* in Sanga Sanga and Tawi Tawi; subspecies *erebina* in Palawan; subspecies *hostilia* in Balabac;

subspecies *martia* in Basilan; subspecies *nargosa* in Dinagat, Homonhon, Leyte, Mindanao, Panaon and Samar. **HABITATS** Flies in forested habitats and can be seen perching on tree-tops or puddling on the ground along forest trails, forest edges and nearby gardens.

Philippine Wanderer ■ *Pareronia boebera* 37–41mm

DESCRIPTION Medium-sized butterfly. Male pale blue with broad black markings on wing margins. Female white with black wing margins and white spots lining submarginal regions of both wings. Undersides of both sexes similar, but paler and silvery in female. **LARVAL FOODPLANTS** *Capparis zeylanica* (Capparaceae family). **DISTRIBUTION** Subspecies *boebera* occurs in Babuyan, Catanduanes, Lubang, Luzon, Marinduque, Pagbilao Grande and Polillo; subspecies *arsamota* in Cebu, Camotes, Masbate, Negros, Palawan, Panay, Romblon, Sibuyan and Ticao; subspecies *bazilana* in Basilan; subspecies *elaitia* in Bohol, Dinagat, Leyte, Panaon and Samar; subspecies *joloana* in Jolo; subspecies *mutya* in Bongao, Sanga Sanga, Sibutu and Tawi Tawi; subspecies *trinobantes* in Mindanao; subspecies *mindorensis* in Lubang and Mindoro. **HABITATS** Flies swiftly in various habitats.

Great Orange Tip ■ *Hebomoia glaucippe* 49–50mm

DESCRIPTION Large, dirty-white butterfly with conspicuous orange markings on apex of forewing. Underside dirty-white with pale brown dusting. **LARVAL FOODPLANTS** *Crateva* and *Capparis* (Capparaceae family). **DISTRIBUTION** Subspecies *philippensis* occurs in Catanduanes, Lubang, Luzon, Marinduque, Mindoro and Polillo; subspecies *boholensis* in Bohol, Cebu, Masbate, Negros, Panay, Siquijor and Ticao; subspecies *cuyonicola* in Cuyo. **HABITATS** Flies gracefully in various habitats, but mostly found in forest edges nectaring on flowering plants.

BRUSHFOOTS, SERGEANTS & SATYRS

Red Lacewing ■ *Cethosia biblis* 38mm

DESCRIPTION Medium-sized butterfly. Sexes look similar, but female has wider hindwing than male. Upperside reddish-orange with black margins broadening at apex, on forewing with median 'needle-tip-like' markings on submarginal region. Underside has submarginal spots on black wing margin. Underside has several markings distinct to genus. Median irregular pale band narrower compared to those of Malay and Luzon Lacewings (p. 32). **LARVAL FOODPLANTS** *Passiflora* and *Adenia* (Passifloraceae family). **DISTRIBUTION** Subspecies *sandakana* occurs in Bongao, Jolo, Sanga Sanga, Sibutu and Tawi Tawi; subspecies *insularis* in Babuyan, Biliran, Bohol, Cebu, Camotes, Leyte, Lubang, Luzon, Marinduque, Masbate, Mindoro, Mindanao (except north-east), Negros, Panay, Samar and Sibuyan; subspecies *placito* in north-east Mindanao; subspecies *liacura* in Balut Island and Sarangani; subspecies *mapuna* in Mapun Island. **HABITATS** Flies in various habitats, including forests and urban gardens.

Malay Lacewing ◾ *Cethosia hypsea* 41mm

DESCRIPTION Medium-sized butterfly. Darker orange than Luzon Lacewing (below). Conspicuous white median band on forewing, originating from mid-costa to space 3 and slightly on space 2; irregular pale yellow band on underside indented at space 4 in hindwing. **LARVAL FOODPLANTS** *Adenia* (Passifloraceae family). **DISTRIBUTION** Subspecies *palawana* occurs in Balabac, Calamian, Dumaran and Palawan. **HABITATS** Although found on western islands of the Philippines, this species also flies in various other habitats.

Luzon Lacewing ◾ *Cethosia luzonica* 37–40mm

DESCRIPTION Medium-sized butterfly. Underside pale yellow median band indented at space 4 of hindwing, and spots on spaces 5 and 6 positioned inwardly, and not in line with band. **LARVAL FOODPLANTS** Plants similar to those for Red and Malay Lacewings (p. 31 and above). **DISTRIBUTION** Subspecies *luzonica* occurs in Luzon; subspecies *boholica* in Biliran, Bohol, Cebu, Leyte, Panaon and Samar; subspecies *magindanaica* in Mindanao; subspecies *pariana* in Guimaras, Masbate, Negros, Panay, Sibuyan and Siquijor. **HABITATS** Flies in various habitats similar to those of Red.

Malayan Cruiser ■ *Vindula dejone* 38–50mm

DESCRIPTION Medium-sized butterfly. Male orange; female brown. Small eye-spots (sometimes one) on tornal region of hindwing. **LARVAL FOODPLANTS** *Passiflora*.
DISTRIBUTION Subspecies *dejone* occurs in Batanes, Bohol, Calamian, Cebu, Dinagat, Leyte, Lubang, Luzon, Marinduque, Masbate, Mindoro, Mindanao, Negros, north Palawan, Panay and Samar.
HABITATS Common butterfly that flies swiftly in various habitats.

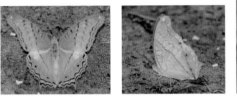

Rustic ■ *Cupha arias* 29–35mm

DESCRIPTION Medium-sized, orange-brown butterfly with black apex on forewing. Conspicuous broad yellow median band with dot on space 2 and large faded black spot on space 1b, or tornal region. **LARVAL FOODPLANTS** Plant genera *Celtis*, *Flacourtia*, *Homalium* and *Lepisanthes*. **DISTRIBUTION** Subspecies *dapatana* occurs in Basilan, Dinagat, Leyte, Mindanao, Panaon and Samar; subspecies *arias* throughout the Philippines, except islands where other subspecies occurs. **HABITATS** Common butterfly, mostly seen in urban areas.

Common Leopard ▪ *Phalanta phalantha* 28–32mm

DESCRIPTION Dark orange with black spots and markings on wings. Common in the Philippines. **LARVAL FOODPLANTS** *Flacourtia jangomas* (Flacourtiaceae family). **DISTRIBUTION** Subspecies *phalantha* occurs throughout the Philippines. **HABITATS** Flies in various habitats, but commonly encountered in lowland areas.

Vagrant ▪ *Vagrans sinha* 30–31mm

DESCRIPTION Medium-sized, dark orange butterfly, with darker orange and black scaling near base towards cell of forewing. Conspicuous black spots on submarginal region of both wings. Underside looks similar but has pinkish-silvery-white composition. **LARVAL FOODPLANTS** *Dellenia*, *Flacourtia* and *Homalium*. **DISTRIBUTION** Subspecies *sinha* occurs throughout the Philippines. **HABITATS** Common species found in various habitats (sometimes seen puddling on the ground).

Common Yeoman ■ *Cirrochroa tyche* 37mm

DESCRIPTION Medium-sized, pale orange butterfly with zigzag markings on submarginal region of both wings. Apex slightly darkened at edges, while hindwing has spots on median region and ends with white spot on costa. Female similar to male, but has whiter median and submarginal regions in both wings. **LARVAL FOODPLANTS** *Hydnocarpus* and *Flacourtia*. **DISTRIBUTION** Subspecies *laudabilis* occurs in Calamian, Dumaran and Palawan; subspecies *languyana* in Tawi Tawi; subspecies *tyche* throughout the Philippines, excluding islands on which other two subspecies occur. **HABITATS** Common in forested habitats.

Satellite Yeoman

■ *Cirrochroa satellita* 33mm

DESCRIPTION Medium-sized orange butterfly with broad black wing margins, and conspicuous bright orange band on median regions. Bases of both wings have orange and black scaling that extends towards median region. Female similar to male, but has paler and brighter orange median band. **LARVAL FOODPLANTS** Probably *Hydnocarpus* and *Flacourtia*. **DISTRIBUTION** Subspecies *illergeta* occurs in Palawan. **HABITATS** Flies in forested areas of Palawan.

Malaysian Assyrian ■ *Terinos clarissa* 39–43mm

DESCRIPTION Medium-sized butterfly. Male has metallic purple band on costa of forewing and half of hindwing. Conspicuous large black patch on forewing, and only on apex of hindwing. Female brown with purple sheen. Undersides of both sexes brown with orange composition. **LARVAL FOODPLANTS** *Caesaria* and *Homalium* (Flacourtiaceae family). **DISTRIBUTION** Subspecies *homonhonensis* occurs in Homonhon; subspecies *lucia* in Palawan; subspecies *luciella* in Balabac; subspecies *lucilla* in Leyte, Luzon, Mindanao and Samar; subspecies *suluensis* in Bongao, Sanga Sanga and Tawi Tawi. **HABITATS** Flies in forested habitats. May also visit nearby home gardens and areas along roadsides.

Painted Lady ■ *Vanessa cardui* 28–30mm

DESCRIPTION Medium-sized orange butterfly with conspicuous white spots near apex and submarginal region of forewing, and three white spots on median near costa forming short band. Irregular black markings near median of forewing, and black circular spots on submarginal of hindwing. Underside similar to upperside but with pinkish-white composition. **LARVAL FOODPLANTS** *Artemisia pallens*, *A. scoparia*, *Blumea balsamifera*, *Debregeasia longifolia* and *Smilax perfoliata*. **DISTRIBUTION** Found in Luzon, Mindanao, Negros and Palawan. **HABITATS** This migratory species has recently been photographed at higher elevations of Baguio in north Luzon.

Blue Admiral ▪ *Kaniska canace* 34–38mm

DESCRIPTION Medium-sized butterfly. Upperside black with conspicuous arching metallic blue band on both wings. Underside looks like burnt leaf. **LARVAL FOODPLANTS** *Smilax* (Smilacaceae family). **DISTRIBUTION** Subspecies *benguetana* occurs in Luzon and north Mindoro; subspecies *oreas* in Panay; subspecies *oplentia* in Mindanao. **HABITATS** Mostly seen at higher elevations.

Common Jester ▪ *Symbrenthia lilaea* 22–26mm

DESCRIPTION Medium-sized butterfly with several black and orange markings on both wings. Square-shaped orange marking on space 4 of forewing, sometimes fused or very close to spots on spaces 5 and 6. Female can be white or pale orange. **LARVAL FOODPLANTS** *Boehmeria* and *Girardinia* (Urticaceae family). **DISTRIBUTION** Subspecies *semperi* occurs throughout the Philippines except Luzon, where subspecies *thimo* occurs. **HABITATS** Common butterfly that flies swiftly in various habitats, but mostly found in forested areas.

Peninsular Jester ▪ *Symbrenthia hippoclus* 22–24mm

DESCRIPTION Medium-sized orange butterfly that looks similar to Common Jester (p. 37), although identity of this species still needs to be studied. Peninsular has more pinkish composition on underside of wings. **LARVAL FOODPLANTS** *Pipturus* (Urticaceae family).
DISTRIBUTION Subspecies *anna* occurs in Bohol, Cebu, Camiguin de Mindanao, Camotes, Dinagat, Leyte, Mindanao, Panaon, Samar and Siargao; subspecies *aritus* in Mapun; subspecies *dissoluta* in Balabac and Palawan; subspecies *galepsus* in Luzon, Marinduque and Mindoro; subspecies *jolonus* in Jolo; subspecies *sperchius* in Basilan.

HABITATS Habitat preferences need further study, since species is common in some islands and rare in others, but it is highly likely that it favours forested habitats.

Himalayan Jester
▪ *Symbrenthia hypselis* 24–25mm

DESCRIPTION Medium-sized butterfly with three distinct irregular orange bands on forewings and two on hindwings. Apex of forewing can have slight orange dusting, and underside marking (scaly black spots) is unique to this species.
LARVAL FOODPLANTS Plants in Urticaceae family.
DISTRIBUTION Subspecies *niphandina* occurs in Palawan.
HABITATS Flies in forested areas of Palawan.

Chocolate Pansy ■ *Junonia iphita* 33mm

DESCRIPTION Medium-sized brown butterfly with greyish-purple sheen on wings. Looks similar to Brown Pansy (below), but eye-spots on median region of hindwing are greatly reduced; also conspicuous dark median band on both wings, which is not pronounced in Brown. **LARVAL FOODPLANTS** Various plants in Acanthaceae family, such as *Justicia*, *Hygrophila*, *Lepidagathis*, *Asteracantha*, *Goldfussia* and *Strobilanthes*. **DISTRIBUTION** Subspecies *adelaida* occurs in Balabac and Palawan. **HABITATS** Common, and mostly found in urban and cleared areas.

Brown Pansy ■ *Junonia hedonia* 30–35mm

DESCRIPTION Medium-sized, chocolate-brown butterfly with forewing cell and cell-end bars. Both wings have several orange-brown eye-spots along submarginal region. **LARVAL FOODPLANTS** *Blechum pyramidatum*, *Ruellia* and *Hemigraphis* (Acanthaceae family). **DISTRIBUTION** Subspecies *ida* occurs throughout the Philippines. **HABITATS** Common and abundant on roadsides, and in open spaces and urban areas. In forested areas prefers to fly near the ground along hiking trails.

Grey Pansy ▪ *Junonia atlites* 28–33mm

DESCRIPTION Medium-sized butterfly that looks similar to Brown Pansy (p. 39) but is greyish, and with eye-spots on both wings. **LARVAL FOODPLANTS** *Nelsonia* and *Hygrophila* (Acanthaceae), and *Limnophila* (Plantaginaceae). **DISTRIBUTION** Subspecies *atlites* occurs throughout the Philippines. **HABITATS** Common in lowland regions, and mostly seen near swampy areas.

Peacock Pansy ▪ *Junonia almana* 27–30mm

DESCRIPTION Medium-sized orange butterfly with eye-spots on spaces 2, 5 and 6 of forewing, and large eye-spot on hindwing and small eye-spot on space 2. **LARVAL FOODPLANTS** *Phyla nodiflora* and *Stachytarpheta jamaicensis* (Verbenaceae), and *Ruellia* (Acanthaceae). **DISTRIBUTION** Subspecies *almana* occurs throughout the Philippines. **HABITATS** Common garden butterfly and abundant in lowland areas, especially in open spaces and shrubby places.

Lemon Pansy ▪ *Junonia lemonias* 26–31mm

DESCRIPTION Medium-sized, dark brown butterfly with eye-spots on space 2 of forewing and space 5 of hindwing. Small, circular yellow spots on forewing, and underside has additional spot on space 5 of forewing and on space 2 of hindwing. **LARVAL FOODPLANTS** Several species in Acanthaceae family, such as *Barleria, Blechum, Dyschoriste, Eranthemum, Hemigraphis, Hygrophila* and *Lepidagathis*. **DISTRIBUTION** Subspecies *janome* occurs in Cebu, Guimaras, Luzon, Marinduque, Mindoro, Negros, Palawan and Panay. **HABITATS** Common in lowland areas, visiting home gardens and flying in open spaces.

Blue Pansy ▪ *Junonia orithya* 23–30mm

DESCRIPTION Medium-sized butterfly. Male has metallic blue on hindwing, and black on base extending towards median region of forewing. Eye-spots on spaces 2 and 5 on forewing in both sexes. Hindwing has eye-spots on spaces 2 and 5, and upperside spots are visible on underside. Smaller spots on spaces 3 and 4 of hindwing. **LARVAL FOODPLANTS** *Antirrhinum majus* (Scrophulariaceae), *Phyla nodiflora* (Verbenaceae), *Striga asiatica* (Scrophulariaceae) and *Stachytarpheta* (Verbenaceae). **DISTRIBUTION** Subspecies *leucasia* occurs throughout the Philippines, except islands of Mapun and Sibutu, where subspecies *metion* occurs. **HABITATS** Common butterfly that flies in various habitats, but mostly found in grassy habitats and also in open spaces.

Lurcher ▪ *Yoma sabina* 40–43mm

DESCRIPTION Large, dark brown to almost black butterfly with conspicuous orange- and purple-tinged band on uppersides of wings. Undersides of wings have silvery composition and median silvery white band. **LARVAL FOODPLANTS** Probably plants in Acanthaceae family, such as *Blechum*. **DISTRIBUTION** Subspecies *podium* found throughout the Philippines. **HABITATS** Common butterfly occasionally seen visiting home gardens.

Malayan Eggfly ▪ *Hypolimnas anomala* 40–48mm

DESCRIPTION Medium to large, dark brown (almost black) butterfly. Wings darker proximally and lighter distally. Series of white dots lined up on submarginal region of both wings, and white spot on hindwing space 7 positioned centrally. **LARVAL FOODPLANTS** *Pipturus* (Urticaceae family). **DISTRIBUTION** Subspecies *anomala* found throughout the Philippines. **HABITATS** Common in forested areas. Can be seen behaving territorially by driving off other butterfly species flying near its territory.

Common Mapwing ■ *Cyrestis maenalis* 26–30mm

DESCRIPTION Medium-sized white butterfly with irregular black lines on both wings. Tornal regions of both wings have orange and black markings. **LARVAL FOODPLANTS** *Ficus ulmifolia* (Moraceae family). **DISTRIBUTION** Subspecies *kynosura* occurs in Bohol, Dinagat, Leyte, Panaon and Samar; subspecies *negros* in Negros. **HABITATS** Flies in forested areas, perching on leaves, or puddling near lake shores or along riversides.

Dark-lined Mapwing ■ *Cyrestis kudrati* 26–30mm

DESCRIPTION Medium-sized butterfly similar to Common Mapwing (above), but with darker and broader bands on both wings. Female much darker than male. **LARVAL FOODPLANTS** Currently unknown, but probably *Ficus* species (Moraceae family). **DISTRIBUTION** Only found in Mindanao. **HABITATS** Has been documented in forested habitats and may exhibit similar behaviour to Common.

Straight-lined Mapwing ■ *Cyrestis nivea* 28–29mm

DESCRIPTION Medium-sized white butterfly with thin lines on wings. Margins have more orange scales compared to other species. Looks almost like the paler version of Common Mapwing (p. 45). **LARVAL FOODPLANTS** Currently unknown, but probably *Ficus* species (Moraceae family). **DISTRIBUTION** Subspecies *superbus* occurs in Palawan and Calamian. **HABITATS** Flies in forested areas and may exhibit similar behaviour to other *Cyrestis* species.

Wavy Maplet ■ *Chersonesia rahria* 19–21mm

DESCRIPTION Medium-sized butterfly. Reddish-orange with narrow black lines. **LARVAL FOODPLANTS** Currently unknown, but probably *Ficus* species (Moraceae family). **DISTRIBUTION** Subspecies *rahria* occurs in Balabac, Palawan, Sanga Sanga, Sibutu and Tawi Tawi. **HABITATS** Flies in forested habitats.

Common Commander ■ *Moduza procris* 30–33mm

DESCRIPTION Medium-sized dark butterfly with reddish composition on wings, especially on submarginal regions. At first glance, shows large white spots on subapex of forewing, with smaller white spot below the two, and tiny, narrow white spots above or along costa. Four large white spots on median region of forewing, and at least seven white spots on median region of hindwing. Underside composition orange, and white spots also present. Female has wider and larger wings than male. **LARVAL FOODPLANTS** Probably *Uncaria* species (Rubiaceae family). **DISTRIBUTION** Subspecies *beckyae* occurs in Balabac; subspecies *pausanias* in Calamian and Palawan; subspecies *liberalis* in Bongao, Sanga Sanga, Sibutu and Tawi Tawi. **HABITATS** Can be seen flying swiftly at forest tree-tops and along forest trails.

Visayan Commander ■ *Moduza jumaloni* 33mm

DESCRIPTION Medium-sized butterfly with black and orange composition and conspicuous white spots lining on median region of forewing. Underside similar to upperside but with bluish-greenish composition. Looks similar to the Clipper butterfly (*Parthenos sylvia*). **LARVAL FOODPLANTS** Possibly plant species of Rubiaceae family. **DISTRIBUTION** Subspecies *jumaloni* occurs in Masbate, Negros and Panay; subpecies *punctata* in Sibuyan. **HABITATS** Flies swiftly along forest trails and forest edges.

Nuyda Commander ■ *Moduza nuydai* 35–40mm

DESCRIPTION Medium-sized, black and orange butterfly, distinguishable by median white band on both wings, which have almost uniform sizes. Red-orange band on submargins of

wings narrower compared with other species. Unique white-bluish zigzag lines on margins of both wings. **LARVAL FOODPLANTS** Currently unknown, but probably plants in Rubiaceae family. **DISTRIBUTION** Subspecies *nuydai* occurs in north and south Luzon; subspecies *hyugai* in Mt Halcon, Mindoro. **HABITATS** Flies in forested habitats and may exhibit similar behaviour to other *Moduza* species.

Palawan Sergeant ■ *Athyma salvini* 25–27mm

DESCRIPTION Medium-sized butterfly similar to Typical Sergeant (opposite). Forewing cell white band in this species reduced to spot near cell end. **LARVAL FOODPLANTS** Currently unknown, but probably *Uncaria* (Rubiaceae) and *Glochidion* (Phyllanthaceae). **DISTRIBUTION** Occurs in Palawan. **HABITATS** Has been seen flying in lowland forest, but may also fly at higher elevations.

Typical Sergeant ■ *Athyma alcamene* 26–30mm

DESCRIPTION Medium-sized, black and white butterfly similar to Kasa Sergeant (p. 50). Differences are that cell streak is continuous and larger near cell end, and there is only one large oblong shape on median region of forewing (two white spots in Kasa); below it is rectangular-shaped white spot, attached to narrower spot below it. Underside similar to upperside, but brighter and some white spots much pronounced. **LARVAL FOODPLANTS** Currently unknown, but probably plants in Rubiaceae and Euphorbiaceae families.

DISTRIBUTION Subspecies *baltazarae* occurs in Cebu, Negros and Panay; subspecies *alcamene* in Basilan, Bohol, Leyte, Mindanao, Panaon and Samar; subspecies *angelesi* in Tawi Tawi; subspecies *generosior* in Mindoro; subspecies *jagori* in Luzon and Marinduque; subspecies *masbatensis* in Masbate.
HABITATS Flies in primary and secondary forests. Can be seen perching on leaf ends, and flying along forest trails and forest edges.

Special Sergeant ■ *Athyma speciosa* 28–32mm

DESCRIPTION Medium-sized, dark orange butterfly with white markings of various sizes along median regions of both wings. White bands broader in male than female, and with bluish tinge or composition. Underside similar but paler. **LARVAL FOODPLANTS** *Flacourtia* species (Flacourtiaceae family). **DISTRIBUTION** Subspecies occurs in Calamian, Cuyo and Palawan; subspecies *preciosa* in Balabac. **HABITATS** Flies in lowland forests and possibly at higher elevations. Takes short flights, then perches on leaf-tips.

Kasa Sergeant ▪ *Athyma kasa* 30–35mm

DESCRIPTION Medium-sized, black and white butterfly with faded white cell-streak ending with white circular spot and triangular white spot on cell end. Three narrow white spots on subapex of forewing and two attached larger white spots on median region. Hindwing black with large white spots attached together, forming band. Underside similar, but brighter and with orange composition. **LARVAL FOODPLANTS** *Antidesma pleuricum* and *Glochidion* (Euphorbiaceae family); may also feed on *Uncaria* (Rubiaceae). **DISTRIBUTION** Subspecies *kasa* occurs in Babuyan, Balesin, Luzon, Marinduque and Polillo; subspecies *bignayana* in Guimaras, Masbate, Negros, Panay, Romblon, Sibuyan and Siquijor; subspecies *epimethis* in Mindoro; subspecies *gordia* in Basilan, Camiguin de Mindanao, Dinagat and Mindanao; subspecies *leyteana* in Leyte and Samar; subspecies *paragordia* in Bohol; subspecies *parakasa* in Cebu and Camotes. **HABITATS** Flies in primary and secondary forests, and can be seen flying in open spaces, on forest trails and at forest edges.

Gutama Sergeant ▪ *Athyma gutama* 29–33mm

DESCRIPTION Medium-sized, black and white butterfly with three distinct, oblong-shaped white markings near subapex of forewing. Cell on forewing has inconspicuous pale white 'trident-shaped' marking. Upper part of median white band forms large, oblong white patch, and hindwing also has distinct and continuous median white band. Underside may look similar, but with more white colouration. **LARVAL FOODPLANTS** *Uncaria*

(Rubiaceae family). **DISTRIBUTION** Subspecies *gutama* occurs in Babuyan, Luzon and Mindoro; subspecies *canlaonensis* in Negros; subspecies *cebuensis* in Cebu; subspecies *sibuyana* in Sibuyan; subspecies *teldeniya* in Balabac, Calamian and Palawan. **HABITATS** Occurs in primary and secondary forests. Usually abundant on forest trails, flying swiftly near host plant.

Knight ■ *Lebadea martha* 29–32mm

DESCRIPTION Medium-sized, reddish-brown butterfly with varying shapes and sizes of white markings. Female similar to male but has broader or larger wings. Underside similar to upperside but paler. **LARVAL FOODPLANTS** Currently unknown, but probably *Ixora* (Rubiaceae family). **DISTRIBUTION** Subspecies *jecieli* occurs in Calamian; subspecies *paulina* in Balabac, Dumaran and Palawan; subspecies *tessellata* in Sibutu; subspecies *undulata* in Sanga Sanga and Tawi Tawi. **HABITATS** Flies in forested areas.

Clipper ■ *Parthenos sylvia* 45–46mm

DESCRIPTION Large, black and orange butterfly with several large white spots on median towards apex of forewing. Some races can have bluish (subspecies *butlerinus*) or yellowish dusting on both wings, and female has relatively broader and wider wings than male. Underside similar to upperside, but with greenish and yellowish composition. **LARVAL FOODPLANTS** Mostly Passifloraceae such as *Adenia* and *Passiflora*. **DISTRIBUTION** Subspecies *philippensis* occurs throughout the Philippines, except islands of Balabac, Bongao, Cuyo, Dumaran, Jolo, Palawan, Sanga Sanga, Siasi, Sibutu and Tawi Tawi; subspecies *butlerinus* in Balabac, Cuyo, Dumaran and Palawan. **HABITATS** Flies in secondary and primary forests. Can be seen flying swiftly at canopy level and nectaring on flowering plants along forest edges or trails.

Lupina Viscount
■ *Tanaecia lupina* 38–47mm

DESCRIPTION Large, dark brown butterfly with conspicuous large white spots on subapical region of forewing. Underside brighter due to greenish composition, and with similar characteristics to upperside. Male smaller than female. **LARVAL FOODPLANTS** Currently unknown, but probably plants in Sapotaceae, Lecythidaceae and Melastomataceae families. **DISTRIBUTION** Subspecies *howarthi* occurs in Negros; subspecies *lupina* in Jolo; subspecies *borromeoi* in Sibuyan; subspecies *panayana* in Panay. **HABITATS** Common forest butterfly that can be seen flying along forest trails and forest edges.

Leucotaenia Viscount ■ *Tanaecia leucotaenia* 34mm

DESCRIPTION Medium-sized, dark brown butterfly with inconspicuous dark brown, oblong-shaped markings on cell of forewing, and conspicuous white band with metallic pale blue scaling on submargin of forewing and median region of hindwing. Underside pale greenish with orange to red composition on forewings; irregular black markings on cell of forewing and near base of hindwing, and white band lined with black spots on both sides. **LARVAL FOODPLANTS** Currently unknown, but probably plants in

Sapotaceae, Lecythidaceae and Melastomataceae families. **DISTRIBUTION** Subspecies *leucotaenia* occurs in Biliran, Bohol, Cebu, Camotes, Leyte, Samar and Panaon; subspecies *aquamarina* in Mindanao; subspecies *cabigoni* in Balut and Sarangani; subspecies *dinorah* in Basilan; subspecies *exul* in Dinagat; subspecies *kulaya* in Homonhon. **HABITATS** Flies in forested areas. Can be seen flying along forest trails and flashing metallic blue colouration on wings.

Short-banded Viscount
■ *Tanaecia aruna* 34–38mm

DESCRIPTION Medium-sized, dark brown butterfly with orange composition. Looks very similar to Pelea Viscount *T. pelea* but has extra column of arrow-shaped markings on median of forewing. Hindwing has several arrow-shaped, pointed markings; underside brighter, with similar characteristics to upperside. **LARVAL FOODPLANTS** Currently unknown, but probably plants in Sapotaceae, Lecythidaceae and Melastomataceae families. **DISTRIBUTION** Subspecies *palawana* occurs in Cuyo, Dumaran and Palawan; subspecies *pallida* in Calamian; subspecies *rudraca* in Balabac. **HABITATS** Flies in forested areas of Palawan.

Streaked Baron ■ *Euthalia alpheda* 30–37mm

DESCRIPTION Medium-sized brown butterfly with inconspicuous, faded, wavy-irregular bands on uppersides of wings. Costa of forewing has greenish composition, and cell of forewing has two distinct, oblong-shaped, dark brown markings. Underside pale brown with white scaling on costa and apex of forewing, and oblong-shaped, black or dark brown markings near bases of both wings. **LARVAL FOODPLANTS** Currently unknown, but probably plants in Loranthaceae and Anacardiaceae families. **DISTRIBUTION** Subspecies *cusama* occurs in Dinagat, Homonhon and Mindanao; subspecies *leytana* in Bohol, Leyte and Samar; subspecies *liaoi* in Negros and Panay; subspecies *mindorensis* in Mindoro; subspecies *phelada* in Luzon; subspecies *rodriguezi* in Palawan; subspecies *sibuyana* in Sibuyan; subspecies *soregina* in Jolo. **HABITATS** Has been seen in forested area, but may also fly in other habitat types.

Philippine Baron
■ *Euthalia lusiada* 30–40mm

DESCRIPTION Medium-sized, dark brown butterfly with greenish tinge or composition on wings. Three inconspicuous dark brown markings on cell of forewing, which are more visible on underside. Underside pale brown with silvery-white dusting or scaling. Female has broader and wider wings than male, which tends to be smaller in size. **LARVAL FOODPLANTS** Currently unknown, but probably plants in Melastomataceae family. **DISTRIBUTION** Subspecies *malissia* occurs in Basilan, Dinagat, Homonhon, Leyte, Mindanao, Panaon and Samar; subspecies *schoenigi* in Negros; subspecies *lusiada* in Babuyan, Luzon and Marinduque; subspecies *mindorana* in Masbate and Mindoro; subspecies *soloni* in Bohol. **HABITATS** Can be seen flying along forest edges and forest trails; also found in cultivated areas.

Blue Baron ■ *Euthalia mahadeva* 30–35mm

DESCRIPTION Medium to large butterfly. Male dark to almost black with conspicuous pale band on margin of forewing, and pale bluish-purplish band on margin of hindwing. Female pale brown with orange composition, and white pointy markings on forewing. **LARVAL FOODPLANTS** Currently unknown, but probably plants in Melastomataceae family. **DISTRIBUTION** Subspecies *rhamases* occurs in Calamian and Palawan; subspecies *dacasini* in Balabac; subspecies *ingae* in Bongao, Sanga Sanga, Sibutu and Tawi Tawi; subspecies *yui* in Dumaran. **HABITATS** Flies in forested habitats.

TOP Male; ABOVE Female; RIGHT Male

54

Common Gaudy Baron
▪ *Euthalia lubentina* 30–34mm

DESCRIPTION Male has two red cell spots with white spot in between; these characteristics much reduced in subspecies *philippensis* in Leyte. White spot on space 2 positioned centrally and slanted towards body. Female larger, with much larger white spots. **LARVAL FOODPLANTS** Currently unknown, but probably plants in Loranthaceae family. **DISTRIBUTION** Subspecies *nadenya* occurs in Luzon and Marinduque; subspecies *philippensis* in Basilan, Bohol, Dinagat, Leyte, Mindanao and Samar; subspecies *goertzi* in Negros and Panay; subspecies *tsukada* in Mindoro. **HABITATS** Mostly seen in primary and secondary forests.

ABOVE Female; TOP RIGHT Male; RIGHT Female

Great Marquis ▪ *Bassarona dunya* 47–50mm

DESCRIPTION Medium to large butterfly. Male dark brown and female paler. Forewing has cell-end spot and another spot (with tiny white spots on both sides) positioned centrally and attached to upper cell vein. Hindwing has tiny spots on spaces 2, 3 and 4, and larger spots on spaces 6 and 7. **LARVAL FOODPLANTS** Currently unknown. **DISTRIBUTION** Subspecies *monara* occurs in Palawan. **HABITATS** Flies in forested areas.

Banded Marquis ▪ *Bassarona teuta* 34–38mm

DESCRIPTION Medium to large butterfly. Male dark brown, and female paler and larger. Tiny white spot on subapical region of forewing and conspicuous line of spots of varying sizes along median of both wings. **LARVAL FOODPLANTS** Currently unknown. **DISTRIBUTION** Subspecies *eson* occurs in Cuyo, Dumaran and Palawan; subspecies *balabacana* in Balabac. **HABITATS** Seen in forested areas of Palawan.

Red-spot Duke ▪ *Dophla evelina* 46–54mm

DESCRIPTION Large butterfly. Upperside dark brown with very conspicuous red spot on forewing cell. Female paler than male. Undersides of both wings similar to uppersides, but with silvery purplish sheen and scaling. **LARVAL FOODPLANTS** Currently unknown,

but probably *Diospyros* (Ebenaceae) and *Anacardium* (Anacardiaceae). **DISTRIBUTION** Subspecies *proditrix* occurs in Basilan, Biliran, Bohol, Camiguin de Mindanao, Dinagat, Leyte, Mindanao and Panaon; subspecies *albusequus* in Sanga Sanga and Tawi Tawi; subspecies *balabacana* in Balabac; subspecies *chloe* in Masbate, Negros, Panay and Sibuyan; subspecies *circe* in Sibutu; subspecies *eva* in Babuyan, Catanduanes, Luzon, Marinduque and Mindoro; subspecies *samarensis* in Samar; subspecies *tyawena* in Calamian, Cuyo, Dumaran and Palawan. **HABITATS** Flies in forested areas and nearby home gardens.

Yellow-tip Archduke ■ *Lexias pardalis* 39–51mm

DESCRIPTION Large butterfly that looks similar to Black-tip Archduke *L. dirtea* but with orange-yellow antennal tips, and hindwing has shiny bluish (greenish tornally) band. Female has several yellow spots scattered throughout wings. **LARVAL FOODPLANTS** *Cratoxylum* (Hypericaceae family). **DISTRIBUTION** Subspecies *cavarna* occurs in Balabac; subspecies *ellora* in Mindoro; subspecies *tethys* in Palawan. **HABITATS** Flies in forested areas, and can be seen puddling on the ground with wings open.

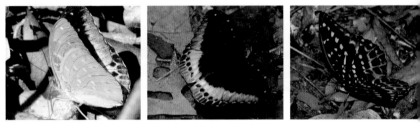

LEFT Male; CENTRE Male; RIGHT Female

Mountain Blue Archduke ■ *Lexias satrapes* 55–61mm

DESCRIPTION Large butterfly. Black with blue tinge on forewing, with series of white spots; hindwing has conspicuous median shiny blue band. Underside dark brown with blue and reddish composition. **LARVAL FOODPLANTS** *Cratoxylum* (Hypericaceae family). **DISTRIBUTION** Subspecies *ormocana* occurs in Leyte and Samar; subspecies *amlana* in Masbate, Negros and west Panay; subspecies *satrapes* in Luzon, Mindoro and Polillo; subspecies *hiwaga* in Camiguin de Luzon; subspecies *ornata* in Sibuyan; subspecies *trapesa* in Mindanao. **HABITATS** Flies near the forest floor, and can also be seen perching on leaves or the ground along trails.

Orange Archduke ■ *Lexias panopus* 38–48mm

DESCRIPTION Male dark brown with dark orange submarginal band broadening towards apex of hindwing and narrowing towards apex of forewing. Underside brown with orange composition and large, greyish-black cell spot. Female has wider and broader wings; submarginal band varies in colour. **LARVAL FOODPLANTS** *Cratoxylum* (Hypericaceae family). **DISTRIBUTION** Subspecies *visayana* occurs in Leyte, Panaon and Samar; subspecies *panopus* in Babuyan and Luzon; subspecies *ingae* in Negros and Panay; subspecies *miscus* in Mindanao; subspecies *boholensis* in Bohol; subspecies *vistrica* in Basilan, Dinagat

and Homonhon. **HABITATS** Rare or common in some months, and can be seen basking along trails. When disturbed, flies swiftly but not too far before perching again.

Common Lascar ■ *Pantoporia hordonia* 23–26mm

DESCRIPTION Black with distinct orange band originating from base towards median region. Orange spots on submarginal region of forewing, and two orange bands on hindwing; median band is wider. Female similar to male, but markings are white, and only narrow bands along submargins of both wings are orange. **FOODPLANTS** Currently unknown, but caterpillar feeds on *Acacia* and *Albizia* (Fabaceae family). **DISTRIBUTION** Subspecies *doronia* occurs in Balabac, Calamian and Palawan; subspecies *maria* in Tawi Tawi. **HABITATS** Prefers to fly in forested habitats.

Dama Lascar ■ *Pantoporia dama* 18–25mm

DESCRIPTION Small, with two subapical spots and rounded spot on space 2. Hindwing median white band narrower in male than in female. In male, cell band narrower, pointy at end and overlaps outside cell end; in female, cell band broadened at tip, forming 'ladle-shape' marking. **LARVAL FOODPLANTS** Currently unknown, but probably *Albizia* (Fabaceae family). **DISTRIBUTION** Subspecies *commixta* occurs in Bohol, Cebu, Camiguin de Mindanao, Dinagat, Leyte, Mindanao, Panaon and Samar; subspecies *dama* in Catanduanes, Luzon, Marinduque, Masbate, Mindoro, Negros, Panay, Romblon and Sibuyan; subspecies *athene* in Balabac, Calamian and Palawan; subspecies *babuyanensis* in Babuyan; subspecies *camotesiana* in Camotes. **HABITATS** Mostly flies in forested areas, especially along trails and forest edges.

Illigera Sailer ■ *Lasippa illigera* 25mm

DESCRIPTION Medium-sized, black and white butterfly with at least three subapical narrow white spots. Cell streak that is not attached to conjoined large spots on spaces 2 and 3. **LARVAL FOODPLANTS** Currently unknown, but probably *Dalbergia* (Fabaceae family). **DISTRIBUTION** Subspecies *hegesias* occurs in Guimaras, Negros and Panay; subspecies *illigera* in north Luzon and Polillo; subspecies *alabatana* in Alabat, Catanduanes, south Luzon, Marinduque and Pagbilao Grande; subspecies *calayana* in Babuyan and Batanes; subspecies *pia* in Basilan; subspecies *sibuyana* in Masbate, Sibuyan and Ticao. **HABITATS** Flies swiftly in forested habitats, and can be seen along forest trails and edges.

Typical Sailer ■ *Neptis mindorana* 24–28mm

DESCRIPTION Medium-sized, black and white butterfly. White spots larger and forewing cell streak broader. Four subapical spots (spots near costa very narrow), and spots on spaces 2 and 3 are almost of the same size. **LARVAL FOODPLANTS** Currently unknown, but probably *Senna*, *Canavalia* and other Fabaceae species. **DISTRIBUTION** Subspecies *ilocana* occurs in Catanduanes, Cebu, Guimaras, Luzon, Marinduque, Masbate, Negros, Panay, Polillo, Sibuyan and Siquijor; subspecies *Mindorana* in Lubang and Mindoro; subspecies *harpasa* in Balabac, Dumaran and Palawan; subspecies *nosba* in Bohol, Camotes, Dinagat, Leyte, Panaon and Samar; subspecies *pseudosoma* in Basilan, Camiguin de Mindanao, Jolo, Mindanao, Sarangani and Siargao. **HABITATS** Flies in forested habitats, and can be seen along forest trails and forest edges.

Constable ■ *Dichorragia nesimachus* 35–40mm

DESCRIPTION Medium-sized, dark green butterfly with series of 'V' shaped markings on margins of both wings. Underside darker, with bluish spots on cell of forewing. **LARVAL FOODPLANTS** Currently unknown, but probably *Meliosma* (Sabiaceae family). **DISTRIBUTION** Subspecies *leytensis* occurs in Leyte and Panaon; subspecies *kawamurai* in Negros and Panay; subspecies *luzonensis* in Luzon and Mindoro; subspecies *machates* in Palawan; subspecies *peisistratus* in Mindanao; subspecies *samarensis* in Samar. **HABITATS** Flies in forested habitats.

Black Prince

■ *Rohana parisatis* 23–24mm

DESCRIPTION Medium-sized butterfly. Male upperside black; female brown with irregular median yellow-white band. Underside in both sexes looks similar to upperside of female. **LARVAL FOODPLANTS** *Celtis philippensis* (Ulmaceae family). **DISTRIBUTION** Subspecies *nana* occurs in Palawan. **HABITATS** Flies in forested habitats, and sometimes visits nearby home gardens for nectar.

Prince

■ *Rohana rhea* 20–25mm

DESCRIPTION Medium-sized butterfly. Male black with at least five tiny white spots near apex of forewing. Female pale brown with orange composition and large white spots on median region of both wings. Undersides of both sexes look the same, but female has large white spots forming median band. **LARVAL FOODPLANTS** *Celtis* species (Cannabaceae family). **DISTRIBUTION** Subspecies *rhea* occurs in Luzon, Marinduque and Pagbilao Grande; subspecies *babuyana* in Camiguin de Luzon; subspecies *danae* in Biliran, Bohol, Leyte, Mindanao, Panaon and Samar; subspecies *dinagatana* in Dinagat; subspecies *mindora* in Mindoro; subspecies *negrosa* in Cebu, Negros, Panay and Sibuyan; subspecies *rana* in Palawan; subspecies *suluana* in Bongao, Sanga Sanga, Sibutu and Tawi Tawi. **HABITATS** Flies in forested habitats, and can be seen nectaring on flowering plants.

Mindanao Circe
▪ *Hestinalis waterstradti* 41–48mm

DESCRIPTION Medium-sized, dark brown butterfly with reddish composition. Forewing has white streaks, originating from base and extending towards median region. Conspicuous elongated reddish patch on cell of forewing. **LARVAL FOODPLANTS** Currently unknown, but probably *Celtis* (Ulmaceae family). **DISTRIBUTION** Subspecies *waterstradti* occurs in south Mindanao; subspecies *borealis* in north Mindanao. **HABITATS** Has been seen in high-elevation forested habitats.

Courtesan ▪ *Euripus nyctelius* 29–39mm

DESCRIPTION Medium-sized butterfly. Male black with several white markings proximally with bluish tinge. Smaller white markings with protrusions on tornal region of hindwings. Space 1b of forewing has purple dusting. Female larger, with wider wings and pale brown vein outlines. Different subspecies have varying markings. **LARVAL FOODPLANTS** Currently unknown, but probably *Trema* (Ulmaceae family). **DISTRIBUTION** Subspecies *sparsus* occurs in Negros and Panay; subspecies *clytia* in Luzon; subspecies *marinduquanus* in Marinduque; subspecies *nysia* in Bohol, Camiguin de Mindanao, Leyte, Mindanao and Samar; subspecies *ophelion* in Balabac; subspecies *arestheion* in Mindoro; subspecies *palawanicus* in Palawan. **HABITATS** Flies in forested habitats.

■ BRUSHFOOTS, SERGEANTS & SATYRS ■

Common Nawab ■ *Polyura athamas* 31–33mm

DESCRIPTION Medium-sized, dark brown butterfly with conspicuous yellow-green median band on both wings, and yellow-green spot on subapical region. Underside silvery-pinkish-brown, with yellow-green band and subapical yellow-green spot. Submarginal region of both wings has crescent-shaped markings. **LARVAL FOODPLANTS** *Acacia*, *Albizia*, *Archidendron*, *Caesalpinia* and *Leucaena*. **DISTRIBUTION** Subspecies *acuta* found throughout the Philippines, except the following islands, which have their own subspecies. Subspecies *angustior* occurs in Bongao, Sanga Sanga and Tawi Tawi; subspecies *kotakaii* in Camiguin de Luzon; subspecies *palawanica* in Calamian, Dumaran and Palawan; subspecies *uraeus* in Balabac and Mapun. **HABITATS** Flies swiftly along forest trails and forest edges, and may also visit nearby gardens.

Jewelled Nawab

■ *Polyura delphis* 49–53mm

DESCRIPTION Large, greenish-yellow butterfly with black marking occupying half of forewing. One or two white spots/dots along subapical regions, and margin of hindwing has short, greenish-black lines. Three tails (middle one shorter), and underside silvery-white with black and orange markings. **LARVAL FOODPLANTS** Currently unknown, but probably *Pithecellobium* (Fabaceae family). **DISTRIBUTION** Subspecies *nivea* occurs in Balabac and Palawan. **HABITATS** Flies in forested habitats.

TOP Female; ABOVE Male

Philippine Rajah
■ *Charaxes amycus* 35–47mm

DESCRIPTION Large butterfly. Male dark orange with broad black margin on forewing and broadening at apex. Hindwing black at apex with series of ocelli on submarginal region. **LARVAL FOODPLANTS** Currently unknown, but probably *Pithecellobium dulce* and *Tamarindus indica*. **DISTRIBUTION** Subspecies *negrosensis* occurs in Negros; subspecies *amycus* in Luzon and Polillo; subspecies *basilium* in Dinagat; subspecies *bayanii* in Marinduque; subspecies *boholensis* in Bohol; subspecies *carolus* in Balut, Camiguin de Mindanao, Mindanao and Sarangani; subspecies *georgius* in Lubang and Mindoro; subspecies *leonides* in north and central Samar; subspecies *leytensis* in Biliran, Leyte and Panaon; subspecies *marion* in Sibuyan; subspecies *shunichii* in Camiguin de Luzon; subspecies *theobaldo* in Masbate and Panay. **HABITATS** Flies in forested habitats, preferring to perch on tree-tops.

Double Eye-spotted Rajah ■ *Charaxes harmodius* 46–51mm

DESCRIPTION Dark orange with black wing margins (broader on forewing apex). Submarginal region of hindwing lined with black spots with tiny white dots/streaks at centre. Female similar to male, but larger or with wider/broader wings. **LARVAL FOODPLANTS** Currently unknown, but probably *Pithecellobium dulce* and *Tamarindus indica*, and may also utilize plants fed on by similar species. **DISTRIBUTION** Subspecies *harpagon* occurs in Calamian and Palawan. **HABITATS** Flies in forested habitats.

Blue Begum ■ *Prothoe francki* 41–43mm

DESCRIPTION Once a subspecies of *P. francki*. Medium-sized butterfly. Both sexes have metallic purple-blue on upperside, three apical spots, and white band from costa towards tornus. Female slightly larger than male. Underside brown with narrow orange markings along margin of forewing. **LARVAL FOODPLANTS** Currently unknown, but probably *Annona* and *Desmos* (Annonaceae family). **DISTRIBUTION** Subspecies *semperi* occurs in Leyte, central and west Mindanao, and Panaon; subspecies *boholensis* in Bohol; subspecies *gregalis* in east Mindanao; subspecies *samarensis* in north Samar. **HABITATS** Flies in forested habitats.

Faun ■ *Faunis phaon* 34–44mm

DESCRIPTION Large butterfly. Upperside brown with yellowish component. Underside dark brown with white dot on apex of forewing, and hindwing has two eye-spots. **LARVAL FOODPLANTS** Plants in Palmae (*Caryota cummnigi*), Musaceae, Liliaceae and Pandanaceae families. **DISTRIBUTION** Subspecies *carfinia* occurs in Guimaras, Masbate, Negros and Panay; subspecies *phaon* in Babuyan and north Luzon; subspecies *pan* in south Luzon and Polillo; subspecies *leucis* in Basilan and Mindanao; subspecies *lurida* in Mindoro; subspecies *sibuyanensis* in Cebu and Sibuyan. **HABITATS** Flies in primary forests. Can be seen flying at ground level along forest trails.

Pale-banded Faun
▪ *Faunis stomphax* 29–35mm

DESCRIPTION Medium to large, dark brown butterfly that looks similar to other *Faunis* species, but has narrow, yellowish irregular line on forewing that originates from costa and terminates towards tornus. **LARVAL FOODPLANTS** Currently unknown, but probably palms. **DISTRIBUTION** Subspecies *plateni* occurs in Balabac, Dumaran and Palawan. **HABITATS** Flies in forested habitats, and can be seen flying at ground level along forest trails.

Silky Owl
▪ *Taenaris horsfieldii* 40–50mm

DESCRIPTION Large, smoky-white butterfly distinguishable by obvious large ocelli on hindwing. **LARVAL FOODPLANTS** Currently unknown, but probably plants in Cycadaceae and Arecaceae families. **DISTRIBUTION** Subspecies *plateni* occurs in Palawan. **HABITATS** Flies in forested habitats of Palawan.

Purple Duffer

■ *Discophora ogina* 48–52mm

DESCRIPTION Large butterfly. Male dark brown with submarginal purple band on both wings. Female yellowish-brown with, on forewing, curved white-purple band (from costa and curving towards tornus). Hindwing has three pale rows of yellow spots; proximal row is the shortest and distal row the longest. **LARVAL FOODPLANTS** Plants in Poaceae and Arecaceae families. **DISTRIBUTION** Subspecies *pulchra* occurs in Masbate, Negros and Panay; subspecies *ogina* in Camiguin de Luzon, Luzon, Marinduque, Mindoro and Polillo. **HABITATS** Flies in forested habitats, and may fly towards nearby gardens.

Common Palm King

■ *Amathusia phidippus* 52–57mm

DESCRIPTION Large butterfly. Both sexes brown to pale brown with brown-yellow wing margins. Underside has brown median terminating on eye-spot at tornal region of hindwing; another eye-spot located at apex. **LARVAL FOODPLANTS** *Cocos nucifera* (Arecaceae family). **DISTRIBUTION** Subspecies *negrosensis* occurs in Negros; subspecies *phidippus* in Balabac, Bongao, Sanga Sanga, Sibutu and Tawi Tawi; subspecies *pollicaris* throughout the Philippines, except islands where other two subspecies occur. **HABITATS** Common in coconut plantations, and also flies into houses, where probably attracted to fruits on tables.

Koh-I-Noor

■ *Amathuxidia amythaon*
57–75mm

DESCRIPTION Large, dark brown butterfly with bluish to purplish (yellow in female) band on forewing. Underside brown with red-pink composition and several dark red lines. Hindwing has eye-spots. **LARVAL FOODPLANTS** Currently unknown. **DISTRIBUTION** Subspecies *philippina* occurs in Leyte, Panaon and Samar; subspecies *negrosensis* in Negros; subspecies *perinthas* in Mindanao. **HABITATS** Flies in forested habitats.

Common Saturn ■

Zeuxidia amythystus 53–59mm

DESCRIPTION Large butterfly. Male dark brown with shiny bluish-violet band on forewing that does not reach tornal region of wing; in hindwing, band narrows halfway before reaching tornus. Female brown with yellow band, but breaks into spots on spaces 2 and 3. Hindwing does not have band. **LARVAL FOODPLANTS** Currently unknown. **DISTRIBUTION** Subspecies *medicieloi* occurs in Biliran, Leyte and Samar; subspecies *sibulana* in Mindanao; subspecies *amethystina* in Camiguin de Mindanao, Dinagat and north to east Mindanao; subspecies *tawiensis* in Sanga Sanga and Tawi Tawi; subspecies *victrix* in Balabac, Cuyo, Dumaran and Palawan. **HABITATS** Flies in forested habitats.

Common Evening Brown
■ *Melanitis leda* 35–38mm

DESCRIPTION Medium-sized butterfly. Generally brown with ocelli on spaces 3 and 4 of forewing. Underside variable – can be pale or dark brown. **LARVAL FOODPLANTS** *Apluda*, *Bambusa* and *Oryza sativa*. **DISTRIBUTION** Subspecies *leda* occurs throughout the Philippines. **HABITATS** Flies at ground level during dusk until dawn. Also common in lowland areas and comes into houses, where probably attracted to fruits.

Evening Brown ■ *Melanitis atrax* 38mm

DESCRIPTION Medium-sized butterfly. Both sexes dark brown. Female has subapical white band, which in male is almost absent or very faded. **LARVAL FOODPLANTS** Currently unknown. **DISTRIBUTION** Subspecies *soloni* occurs in Masbate, Negros and Panay; subspecies *atrax* in Alabat, Babuyan, Burias, Luzon, Marinduque and Polillo;

subspecies *bazilana* in Basilan; subspecies *cajetana* in Bohol, Cebu and Camotes; subspecies *elya* in Jolo; subspecies *erichsonia* in Mindoro; subspecies *lucillus* in Camiguin de Mindanao, Dinagat, Mindanao and Sarangani; subspecies *sibuyana* in Sibuyan; subspecies *semperi* in Biliran, Leyte, Panaon and Samar; subspecies *oliver* in Sanga Sanga, Sibutu and Tawi Tawi. **HABITATS** Flies in forested habitats. Can also be seen flying on cultivated land near forests.

Parce Palmfly ▪ *Elymnias parce* 32–38mm

DESCRIPTION Medium-sized butterfly. Sexes look similar but female paler than male. Male upperside almost black with rusty-brown wing margins. Underside hindwing has conspicuous submarginal spots. **LARVAL FOODPLANTS** Currently unknown, but probably certain palm species. **DISTRIBUTION** Subspecies *parce* occurs in Balabac, Dumaran and Palawan; subspecies *justini* in Calamian. **HABITATS** Flies in forested habitats and nearby gardens.

Sansoni's Palmfly ▪ *Elymnias sansoni* 40–44mm

DESCRIPTION Medium-sized butterfly. Male almost black with series of submarginal white spots. Forewing apical white spots larger. Female pale brown with interveinal white streaks with enlarged tips. **LARVAL FOODPLANTS** Currently unknown, but probably certain palm species. **DISTRIBUTION** Subspecies *sansoni* occurs in Cebu and Negros; subspecies *aklanensis* in Panay. **HABITATS** Flies in forested habitats. Can be seen perching and flying along forest trails and forest edges.

Malayan Owl
▪ *Neorina lowii* 54–60mm

DESCRIPTION Large butterfly. Male dark brown and female paler. Conspicuous yellow patches on both wings: on tornal region of forewing and on apex of hindwing (larger). White dots on forewing spaces 2 and 3; other spots positioned at opposite ends of subapical ocellus. LARVAL FOODPLANTS Certain plants in Graminae family. DISTRIBUTION Subspecies *princesa* occurs in Balabac and Palawan. HABITATS Flies in forested habitats.

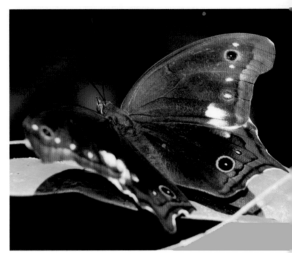

Northern Wallacean ▪ *Zethera pimplea* 40–43mm

DESCRIPTION Medium to large butterfly. Male has narrower wings than female; dark brown, with distinct large white band. Same characteristics on underside. Female darker, with broader venation compared to that of other female species in genus. LARVAL FOODPLANTS *Dinochloa scandens* (Graminae family). DISTRIBUTION Subspecies *pimplea* found in Babuyan, Burias, Catanduanes, Camiguin de Luzon, Luzon, Marinduque and Polillo; subspecies *gadrosia* in Mindoro. HABITATS Flies in forested habitats.

Central Wallacean ■ *Zethera musides* 40–45mm

DESCRIPTION Medium to large butterfly. Male dark brown with submarginal spots on forewing that become wider at tornus (spaces 1a and 1b). Hindwing has large median band similar to that of Northern Wallacean (p. 71). Female white and looks similar to Eastern Wallacean Z. *thermaea*, but cell-end black spot larger and marginal markings shorter. **LARVAL FOODPLANTS** Plants in Graminae family, including *Arundinaria*. **DISTRIBUTION** Found in Cebu, Guimaras, Masbate, Negros, Panay, Siquijor and Ticao. **HABITATS** Prefers to fly in forested habitats, and can be seen along riverbanks. Exhibits territorial behaviour.

LEFT Male; CENTRE Female; RIGHT Male

Bamboo Treebrown ■ *Lethe europa* 33–35mm

DESCRIPTION Medium-sized butterfly; variable, especially in males. Male usually dark brown with two subapical white spots that are sometimes not well pronounced. Indonesian race has metallic purple overlaid on wings. Underside dark brown with series

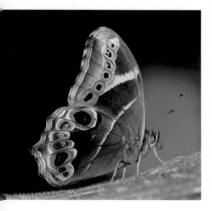

of ocelli (more like ringlets on forewing) on submarginal region. Largest ocellus at space 6. Median white or yellow narrow band. In female, upperside has white median band that originates on costa and extends towards close to tornus. Submarginal spots enlarged, with dark dusting inside. **LARVAL FOODPLANTS** Mostly plants in Graminae family, which includes *Bambusa*. **DISTRIBUTION** Subspecies *alaca* occurs in Balabac, Calamian, Dumaran and Palawan; subspecies *acutefascia* in Sanga Sanga, Sibutu and Tawi Tawi; subspecies *cevanna* throughout the Philippines, except islands where other two subspecies occur. **HABITATS** Swift flying, preferring to fly at canopy level and perching on leaves or branches.

Lorquin's Satyr ■ *Ptychandra lorquinii* 28–31mm

DESCRIPTION Medium-sized butterfly. Male metallic blue with white subapical spot and brand near base of forewing. Underside dark brown with reddish composition and series of submarginal ocelli, with at least three on forewing and seven on hindwing. Female pale brown with white median band that is slightly conjoined to white spot on space 3. Also circular spot on space 4. Large ocellus near costa of hindwing. **LARVAL FOODPLANTS** *Dinochloa* and *Bambusa* (both Graminae family). **DISTRIBUTION** Subspecies *lorquinii* occurs in Camiguin de Luzon, Luzon, Marinduque, Mindoro and Polillo; subspecies *bazilana* in Basilan; subspecies *boholensis* in Bohol; subspecies *leytensis* in Biliran, Leyte and Samar; subspecies *plateni* in Mindanao, Sarangani and Siargao. **HABITATS** Fast-flying butterfly that prefers to fly in forested habitats and nearby gardens. Notable for metallic blue on uppersides of wings, which flashes when flying.

LEFT Male; CENTRE Female; RIGHT Male

Nigger

■ *Orsotriaena medus* 22–25mm

DESCRIPTION Medium-sized, dark brown butterfly with narrow white band on underside, and ocelli on spaces 2 and 5 on forewing, and spaces 2, 5 and 6 (smaller) on hindwing. **LARVAL FOODPLANTS** Several Graminae species, such as *Oryza sativa*. **DISTRIBUTION** Subspecies *medus* occurs throughout the Philippines. **HABITATS** Very common butterfly in grassy environments and on cultivated land.

Tagala Bushbrown ■ *Culapa tagala* 28–31mm

DESCRIPTION Medium-sized, dark brown butterfly that is paler proximally, with visible ocelli on space 2 of forewing and space 2 of hindwing. Underside darker, with ocelli on space 2 and two ocelli on subapical region of forewing. Ocelli on space 2 and apex of

hindwing larger than ocelli on spaces 1b, 4 and 5. **LARVAL FOODPLANTS** Plants in Gramineae family. **DISTRIBUTION** Subspecies *venostes* occurs in Bohol, Leyte, Panaon and Samar; subspecies *tagala* in Burias, Luzon and Marinduque; subspecies *hernica* in Jolo, Sanga Sanga and Tawi Tawi; subspecies *mataurus* in Guimaras, Masbate, Negros, Panay and Ticao; subspecies *mindorana* in Mindoro; subspecies *palawana* in Balabac and Palawan; subspecies *semirasa* in Basilan, Mindanao and Sarangani. **HABITATS** Common butterfly that flies in various habitats, including forest trails and forest edges, and in lowland areas.

Bisaya Bushbrown
■ *Culapa bisaya* 25mm

DESCRIPTION Medium-sized, dark brown butterfly with eye-spot near tornus of forewing and another near tornus of hindwing. Underside has tiny eye-spot near apex of forewing and another one near tornus. Eye-spot near apex of hindwing larger than 2–3 eye-spots below it, but almost the same size as eye-spot near tornus and a smaller one below it. **LARVAL FOODPLANTS** Currently unknown, but probably certain grass species (Poaceae). **DISTRIBUTION** Subspecies *bisaya* occurs in Babuyan, Burias, Luzon, Marinduque and Polillo; subspecies *baboy* in Leyte; subspecies *samina* in Mindoro. **HABITATS** Flies in various habitats, such as forests and lowland grassy areas.

Common Bushbrown ■ *Mycalesis perseus* 21–24mm

DESCRIPTION Medium-sized, dark brown butterfly with eye-spots on submarginal region. Underside has series of submarginal ocelli, and ocellus on space 2 of hindwing is positioned inwardly, not aligned with other ocelli. **LARVAL FOODPLANTS** Plants in Gramineae family. **DISTRIBUTION** Subspecies *caesonia* occurs in Bohol, Cebu, Leyte, Luzon, Mindoro, Mindanao, Negros and Panay; subspecies *acarya* in Jolo and Palawan. **HABITATS** Common butterfly that flies in various habitats, including forest trails and forest edges, and lowland areas.

Dark-branded Bushbrown ■ *Mycalesis mineus* 22–25mm

DESCRIPTION Medium-sized, dark brown butterfly with eye-spots on submarginal region. Underside looks similar to that of Common Bushbrown (above) but eye-spot on space 2 of hindwing is aligned with other ocelli. **LARVAL FOODPLANTS** *Pogonatherum* and *Thysanolaena*. **DISTRIBUTION** Subspecies *philippina* occurs in Alabat, Bohol, Camotes, Cuyo, Guimaras, Jolo, Luzon, Mindoro, Negros, Palawan and Sibuyan; subspecies *macromalayana* in Mapun. **HABITATS** Common butterfly that flies in various habitats, including forest trails and forest edges, and in lowland areas. See Igoleta Bushbrown (p. 76).

Igoleta Bushbrown ▪ *Mycalesis igoleta* 21–27mm

DESCRIPTION Medium-sized, dark brown butterfly with well-pronounced ocellus on space 2. Underside similar to that of Common and Dark-branded Bushbrowns (p. 75), but median pale band is broader on hindwing and ocellus on space 2 of forewing is larger and almost attached to median band. **LARVAL FOODPLANTS** Gramineae such as *Digitaria*. **DISTRIBUTION** Subspecies *negrosensis* occurs in Bohol, Cebu, Guimaras, Masbate, Negros, Panay, Romblon, Sibuyan and Siquijor; subspecies *igoleta* in Alabat, Babuyan, Batanes, Leyte, Luzon, Marinduque and Samar; subspecies *mangyan* in Mindoro. **HABITATS** Common butterfly that flies in various habitats, including forest trails and forest edges, and in lowland areas. Also flies with Common and Dark-branded.

Purple Bushbrown
▪ *Mycalesis orseis* 25mm

DESCRIPTION Medium-sized, dark brown butterfly. Underside has conspicuous white median submarginal bands on both wings; submarginal region with eye-spots has bright yellow-orange composition. **LARVAL FOODPLANTS** Currently unknown, but probably plants in Graminae family. **DISTRIBUTION** Subspecies *flavotincta* occurs in Balabac and Palawan. **HABITATS** Flies in various habitats.

Janardana Bushbrown
■ *Mycalesis janardana* 22–23mm

DESCRIPTION Medium-sized brown butterfly that looks similar to other *Mycalesis* species, but has single eye-spot near apex of forewing with very large eye-spot below. On hindwing, series of seven eye-spots are lined up together on submarginal region. Two eye-spots (third and fourth from bottom) relatively larger compared to other five eye-spots. **LARVAL FOODPLANTS** Currently unknown, but probably plants in Graminae family. **DISTRIBUTION** Subspecies *circella* occurs in Bohol, Leyte and Panaon; subspecies *micromede* in Basilan, Mindanao and Sarangani. **HABITATS** Flies in various habitats, including forests and nearby home gardens.

Eyed Cyclops ■
Erites argentina 24–25mm

DESCRIPTION Medium-sized brown butterfly with large eye-spot on tornus of forewing. Also conspicuous dark orange bands, one forming 'U' shape on hindwing. **LARVAL FOODPLANTS** Currently unknown. **DISTRIBUTION** Subspecies *ochreana* found in Balabac, Calamian, Dumaran and Palawan. **HABITATS** Flies in forested areas, and prefers to fly at ground level in shaded habitats.

Luzon Striped Ringlet
▪ *Ragadia luzonia* 20–23mm

DESCRIPTION Medium-sized butterfly with 'zebra-like' patterns on wings. Underside has two black bands and another band with ring-like markings on submarginal region of wings. Ring-like markings on hindwing include four larger ones, and markings near anal outlined with orange scales. **LARVAL FOODPLANTS** *Selaginella* (Selaginellaceae family), a clubmoss species. **DISTRIBUTION** Subspecies *luzonia* occurs in Alabat, Luzon, Marinduque and Polillo; subspecies *luteofasciata* in Sibuyan; subspecies *masbatensis* in Masbate; subspecies *negrosensis* in Negros; subspecies *obscura* in Catanduanes; subspecies *treadawayi* in west Panay. **HABITATS** Flies in forested habitats, and can be seen along forest trails and forest edges. Mostly prefers to perch on ferns.

Palawan Striped Ringlet ▪ *Ragadia maganda* 20–23mm

DESCRIPTION Medium-sized butterfly that looks similar to Luzon Striped Ringlet (above), but has faded narrow black bands on underside. Silvery eye-spots (ocelli) on margins of both wings have orange composition. **LARVAL FOODPLANTS** *Selaginella* (Selaginellaceae family), a clubmoss species. **DISTRIBUTION** Found in Palawan. **HABITATS** Flies in forested habitats, and can be seen perching on ferns.

Mindanao Striped Ringlet
■ *Ragadia melindena* 22mm

DESCRIPTION Medium-sized butterfly that looks similar to Luzon Striped Ringlet (opposite), but has median black band that narrows in middle, and four fused hindwing ringlets are positioned inwards (centered in Luzon). **LARVAL FOODPLANTS** *Selaginella* (Selaginellaceae family), a clubmoss species. **DISTRIBUTION** Subspecies *melindena* occurs in Camiguin de Mindanao, Mindanao and Sarangani; subspecies *basilensis* in Basilan; subspecies *boholensis* in Bohol; subspecies *kakahuyan* in Leyte and Samar. **HABITATS** Flies in forested habitats, and may exhibit similar behaviour to the other species.

Negros Pale Ringlet ■ *Acrophtalmia yamashitai* 15–17mm

DESCRIPTION Small butterfly that looks similar to Luzon Pale Ringlet (p. 80), but has broader dark brown wing margins. Additional three reduced hindwing ocelli just above large tornal ocellus sometimes absent. **LARVAL FOODPLANTS** *Selaginella* (Selaginellaceae family), a clubmoss species. **DISTRIBUTION** Occurs in Negros and Panay. **HABITATS** Flies with *Ragadia* species, and can be seen flying weakly in shaded areas of forests.

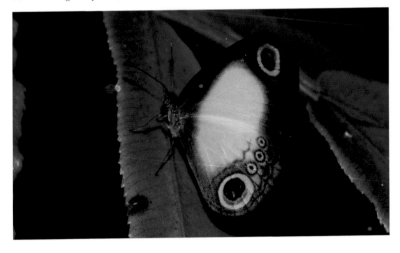

Luzon Pale Ringlet ■ *Acrophtalmia luzonica* 15mm

DESCRIPTION Small, dark brown butterfly with very large white band on both wings. Large eye-spot on apex of forewing and another one on tornus of hindwing; three other smaller eye-spots above it, and zigzag line along median region. **LARVAL FOODPLANTS** *Selaginella* (Selaginellaceae family), a clubmoss species. **DISTRIBUTION** Occurs in north Luzon. **HABITATS** Flies weakly along forest floor and favours shaded microhabitats.

Common Five-ring ■ *Ypthima stellera* 15–17mm

DESCRIPTION Small, dark brown butterfly with large ocellus on forewing just beyond cell. Underside hindwing has three pairs of ocelli; a pair on spaces 1b, 2, 3, 5 and 6. **LARVAL FOODPLANTS** *Digitaria radicosa* (Graminae family). **DISTRIBUTION** Subspecies *stellera* occurs in Babuyan, Basilan, Bohol, Cebu, Camiguin de Mindanao, Camotes, Dinagat, Jolo, Luzon, Leyte, Marinduque, Mindoro, Mindanao, Negros, Panay, Panaon, Romblon, Samar and Siargao. **HABITATS** Very common and abundant in lowland areas, especially in disturbed habitats and on cultivated land. Also common along forest trails and forest edges.

Common Three-ring ■ *Ypthima sempera* 20mm

DESCRIPTION Small, dark brown butterfly that looks similar to Common Five-ring (opposite) on upperside but with ocelli on spaces 1b and 2 on hindwing. Underside of forewing darker compared to hindwing, and additional ocellus near apex. **LARVAL FOODPLANTS** Grass species that include *Bambusa*, *Paspalum* and *Digitaria* (Poaceae family). **DISTRIBUTION** Subspecies *sempera* occurs in Alabat, Bohol, Cebu, Camotes, Guimaras, Leyte, Luzon, Marinduque, Masbate, Mindoro, Negros, Panay, Panaon and Samar. **HABITATS** Common and abundant butterfly that flies with Common Five-ring. Can be seen in lowland areas, on cultivated land, and along forest trails and forest edges.

Yellow Glassy Tiger ■ *Parantica aspasia* 39–44mm

DESCRIPTION Medium-sized butterfly. Male has narrower wings than female, which has broader and rounded wings. Space 1b of forewing yellow, as well as proximal region of hindwing. **LARVAL FOODPLANTS** Probably *Raphistemma* (Apocynaceae family). **DISTRIBUTION** Subspecies *cerilla* occurs in Balabac, Calamian and Palawan; subspecies *flymbra* in Dumaran. **HABITATS** Flies in forested habitats.

Common Glassy Tiger ▪ *Parantica vitrina* 32–38mm

DESCRIPTION Medium-sized butterfly with clear wing. Male has broad black scaling on tornal region of hindwing. Female has faded, short black streaks on spaces 2 and 3 of forewing. **LARVAL FOODPLANTS** Several plants in Asclepiadaceae family, including *Gymnema, Ceropegia, Cynanchum, Marsdenia, Tylophora* and *Vincetoxicum*. **DISTRIBUTION** Subspecies *oenone* occurs in Bohol, Cebu, Leyte, Mindanao, Negros, Panay and Samar; subspecies *vitrina* in Babuyan, Batanes, Luzon, Marinduque and Mindoro. **HABITATS** Flies in primary and secondary forests, and can be seen along forest edges and forest trails. May sometimes fly in home gardens in lowland areas.

Luzon Glassy Tiger

▪ *Parantica luzonensis* 40mm

DESCRIPTION Medium-sized, dark brown butterfly with white markings and streaks. Male has broad black scaling on tornus of hindwing. White streaks on spaces 5 and 6 of forewing are long, narrowing in the middle. **LARVAL FOODPLANTS** *Tylophora* (Asclepiadaceae family). **DISTRIBUTION** Subspecies *simonides* occurs in Balabac and Palawan; subspecies *luzonensis* throughout the Philippines, except islands where other subspecies occurs. **HABITATS** Flies in primary and secondary forests.

Dark Blue Glassy Tiger ■ *Ideopsis vulgaris* 40mm

DESCRIPTION Semi-transparent, medium-sized butterfly. White rectangular spots on spaces 2 and 3 of forewing pointy at their lower edges facing base of wing. Hindwing cell has dark conjoined black streak. **LARVAL FOODPLANTS** *Gymnema*, and may also include *Parsonsia* (Asclepiadaceae family). **DISTRIBUTION** Subspecies *palawana* occurs in Balabac, Calamian, Dumaran and Palawan. **HABITATS** Flies in primary and secondary forests.

Grey Glassy Tiger ■ *Ideopsis juventa* 36–43mm

DESCRIPTION Medium-sized butterfly that looks similar to Dark Blue Glassy Tiger (above), but has broader black markings on forewing cell. Spots on spaces 2 and 3 larger, and hindwing cell has very pale, conjoined black streak. **LARVAL FOODPLANTS** *Gymnema* (Asclepiadaceae), *Piper* (Piperaceae) and *Telosma* (Asclepiadaceae).

DISTRIBUTION Subspecies *kinitis* occurs in Balabac, Calamian, Mapun and Palawan; subspecies *luzonica* in Babuyan and Batanes; subspecies *suluana* in Bongao, Jolo, Sanga Sanga, Siasi, Sibutu and Tawi Tawi; subspecies *manillana* throughout the Philippines, except islands where other subspecies occur. **HABITATS** Flies in various habitats, including forests, and down to lower elevations with home gardens and cultivated land.

Smaller Wood Nymph ■ *Ideopsis gaura* 50mm

DESCRIPTION Medium-sized butterfly with very narrow forewing, especially in male; several black spots throughout wings. Male has broader black markings on costa of forewing compared to female. **LARVAL FOODPLANTS** *Melodinus* (Apocynaceae family). **DISTRIBUTION** Subspecies *canlaonii* occurs in Negros; subspecies *anapina* in Leyte, Mindoro and Samar; subspecies *anapis* in Luzon and Marinduque; subspecies *panayana* in Panay; subspecies *cesa* in Calamian and Palawan. **HABITATS** Flies in primary and secondary forests, and can be seen flying slowly along forest trails and forest edges.

Dark Blue Tiger ■ *Tirumala hamata* 46mm

DESCRIPTION Medium-sized butterfly that looks similar to Narrow Dark Blue Tiger *T. septentrionis* but inner large white spot on space 1b is pointy facing base of wing. Dark brown marking on cell of hindwing separated or diverged at cell end. **LARVAL FOODPLANTS** Plants in Asclepiadaceae and Apocynaceae families. **DISTRIBUTION** Subspecies *nephthys* occurs in Jolo, Sanga Sanga, Sibutu and Tawi Tawi; subspecies *pelagia* in Cuyo; subspecies *tibula* in Camotes; subspecies *orientalis* throughout the Philippines, except islands where other subspecies occur. **HABITATS** Flies in various habitats, including montane forests and places towards lowland areas.

Plain Tiger ■ *Danaus chrysippus* 34–35mm

DESCRIPTION Medium-sized orange butterfly. Upper half of forewing dark brown with spots. Male has broad black scaling on space 1b or along vein 2 of hindwing. **LARVAL FOODPLANTS** Plants in Asclepiadaceae family. **DISTRIBUTION** Subspecies *chrysippus* occurs throughout the Philippines. **HABITATS** Flies in various habitats, but commonly found in home gardens and open fields with bushes.

White Tiger ■ *Danaus melanippus* 38–45mm

DESCRIPTION Medium-sized butterfly that looks similar to Plain Tiger (above), but white and with dark brown venation. **LARVAL FOODPLANTS** Probably plants in Asclepiadaceae family. **DISTRIBUTION** Subspecies *mezentius* occurs in Balabac; subspecies *Philozigetes* in south-east Mindanao and Sarangani; subspecies *edmondii* throughout the Philippines, except in areas and islands where other subspecies occur. **HABITATS** Flies in various habitats, but prefers to fly in shaded habitats and also visits nearby home gardens.

Common Tiger ■ *Danaus genutia* 39–40mm

DESCRIPTION Medium-sized orange butterfly with black wing margins occupying half of forewing, and subapex has five large white markings. Wing veins outlined in black.

LARVAL FOODPLANTS *Cynanchum* and *Asclepias* (Apocynaceae family). **DISTRIBUTION** Subspecies *genutia* occurs in Balabac, Bugsuk and Palawan; subspecies *adnana* throughout the Philippines, except the three islands where other subspecies occurs. **HABITATS** Flies in various habitats, including forests and lowland urbanized areas.

Schaus's Crow ■ *Euploea blossomae* 47–50mm

DESCRIPTION Medium-sized black butterfly with white spots arching on forewing. Spots on subapex relatively larger (except in subspecies in Mindoro) compared to others.

Some subspecies can have bluish metallic colouration when viewed at a certain angle. Subspecies in Mindoro has broader white markings on both wings. **LARVAL FOODPLANTS** Probably plants in Moraceae and Apocynaceae families. **DISTRIBUTION** Subspecies *blossomae* occurs in north and south Luzon; subspecies *corazonae* in Negros and Panay; subspecies *escapardae* in south Palawan; subspecies *hilongenis* in north-east Mindanao; subspecies *sibulanensis* in Mindanao; subspecies *tamaraw* in north Mindoro. **HABITATS** Rarely photographed, and mostly flies in primary and secondary forests.

Swainson's Crow

■ *Euploea swainson* 42–47mm

DESCRIPTION Medium-sized black butterfly with white spots on both wings that vary in size depending on subspecies. **LARVAL FOODPLANTS** Probably plants in Moraceae and Apocynaceae families. **DISTRIBUTION** Subspecies *swainson* occurs in Catanduanes, north-east, central and south Luzon, Marinduque and Sibuyan; subspecies *butra* in Calamian, Cuyo, Dumaran and Palawan; subspecies *donovani* in Mindanao; subspecies *duplex* in Basilan; subspecies *jadiva* in Balabac; subspecies *panayensis* in Panay; subspecies *suluana* in Bongao, Jolo, Sanga Sanga, Sibutu and Tawi Tawi. **HABITATS** Flies in lowland forests.

Blue King Crow ■ *Euploea camaralzeman* 47–57mm

DESCRIPTION Medium-sized butterfly. Male dark brown with two columns of submarginal white spots on both wings. Female paler with more white spots throughout wings. **LARVAL FOODPLANTS** *Strophanthus* (Apocynacae family). **DISTRIBUTION** Subspecies *claudina* occurs in Calamian and Palawan; subspecies *cratis* in Babuyan, Batanes, Fuga and north Luzon. **HABITATS** Flies in forested habitats.

Striped Blue Crow ■ *Euploea mulciber* 50–53mm

DESCRIPTION Medium-sized butterfly. Male has narrow brand on upperside part of cell of hindwing. Lower half of hindwing reddish-brown; upper half brown. Underside of male has white spot on space 2 positioned centrally or near cell end. Several subspecies, and both sexes have varying forms. **LARVAL FOODPLANTS** *Ficus* (Moraceae), *Nerium* and *Toxocarpus* (Apocynaceae). **DISTRIBUTION** Subspecies *visaya* occurs in Biliran, Bohol, Camotes, Leyte, Panaon and Samar; subspecies *cebuensis* in Cebu; subspecies *dufresne* in Luzon and Polillo; subspecies *kochi* in Negros and Panay; subspecies *paupera* in Balabac, Calamian, Dumaran and Palawan; subspecies *mindanensis* in Mindanao; subspecies *barsine* in Batanes; subspecies *dinagatensis* in Dinagat; subspecies *guimarasensis* in Guimaras; subspecies *masbatensis* in Masbate; subspecies *portia* in Sibutu; subspecies *semperi* in Lubang and Mindoro; subspecies *seraphita* in Basilan and Jolo; subspecies *subvisaya* in Marinduque; subspecies *tawitawiensis* in Bongao, Sanga Sanga and Tawi Tawi; subspecies *ticaoana* in Ticao; subspecies *triggia* in Romblon and Sibuyan. **HABITATS** Flies mostly in forested habitats, and can be seen nectaring on flowers along forest trails and forest edges.

Dwarf Crow ■ *Euploea tulliolus* 30–35mm

DESCRIPTION Medium-sized butterfly. Male dark brown with shiny blue-purple on forewing; female paler. White bands on subapical of forewing, which turn into white spots towards tornus. Submarginal spots on hindwing can be absent in some individuals. **LARVAL FOODPLANTS** *Nerium* (Apocynaceae), and may also utilize *Ficus* (Moraceae). **DISTRIBUTION** Subspecies *pollita* occurs in Babuyan, Bohol, Cebu, Camiguin de Mindanao, Camotes, Dinagat, Guimaras, Leyte, Luzon, Marinduque, Masbate, central and north Mindoro, Mindanao (except south-west), Negros, north-east Panay, Panaon, Samar, Sibuyan and Ticao; subspecies *aristotelis* in Bongao, Sanga Sanga, Sibutu and Tawi Tawi; subspecies *monilina* in Basilan, Jolo and south-west Mindanao; subspecies *palawana*

in Balabac, Calamian, Cuyo, Dumaran, south Mindoro, Palawan and west Panay. **HABITATS** Mostly flies in forested areas, and can also be seen on riverbanks in barren lowland areas.

Blue-branded King Crow ■ *Euploea eunice* 40–55mm

DESCRIPTION Variable, medium-sized butterfly. Male has broad black scaling on space 1b of forewing and overlapping androconial patch on cell of hindwing. Female has double white-bluish bands on space 1b of forewing. **LARVAL FOODPLANTS** Probably plants in Moraceae and Apocynaceae families. **DISTRIBUTION** Subspecies *syra* occurs in Balabac, Calamian, Palawan and Tawi Tawi; subspecies *oculata* occurs throughout the Philippines, except islands where other subspecies occurs. **HABITATS** Flies in primary and secondary forests.

Paper Kite ■ *Idea leuconoe* 55–75mm

DESCRIPTION Large white butterfly with yellowish composition and heavily marked with black spots. Median region of hindwing has arrow-shaped markings. **LARVAL FOODPLANTS** *Parsonsia* (Apocynaceae family). **DISTRIBUTION** Subspecies *leuconoe* occurs in Alabat, Catanduanes and Luzon; subspecies *atheis* in Polillo; subspecies *esanga* in Balut and Sarangani; subspecies *jumaloni* in Cebu; subspecies *gordita* in Marinduque, Masbate, Mindoro, Negros, Panay, Romblon and Sibuyan; subspecies *nigriana* in Balabac and Taganac; subspecies *sibutana* in Sanga Sanga, Sibutu and Tawi Tawi; subspecies *obscura* in Basilan, Dinagat, Homonhon, Mindanao and Siargao; subspecies *princesa* in Palawan; subspecies *samara* in Biliran, Bohol, Leyte and Samar; subspecies *solyma* in Babuyan and Batanes. **HABITATS** Flies in various habitats, including forests and lowland areas.

White-spotted Beak

▪ *Libythea narina* 24–26mm

DESCRIPTION Medium-sized, dark brown butterfly with yellow-orange dusting proximally on forewings. At least four subapical white spots, distal cell spot and circular spot on space 2. Hindwing has narrow yellow median band, usually composed of four spots. **LARVAL FOODPLANTS** Currently unknown, but probably *Celtis* (Cannabaceae family). **DISTRIBUTION** Subspecies *luzonica* occurs in Luzon, north Mindoro, Negros, Palawan and Panay. **HABITATS** Flies in forested habitats.

Blue Beak ▪ *Libythea geoffroy* 28mm

DESCRIPTION Medium-sized butterfly. Male dark brown with purple sheen; subapical spots much more visible on underside. Female paler, with orange-brown hindwings. Spot on forewing space 2 large and usually attached to tiny spot on space 3. Cell spot and subapical spots are present; inconspicuous orange median band on hindwing. **LARVAL FOODPLANTS** *Celtis philippensis* (Cannabaceae family). **DISTRIBUTION** Subspecies *bardas* occurs in Cebu, Luzon, Marinduque, Mindoro, Negros and Panay; subspecies *philippina* in Bohol, Bongao, Camiguin de Mindanao, Leyte, Mindanao, Palawan, Panaon, Samar, Sibutu and Tawi Tawi. **HABITATS** Flies in forested habitats.

BLUES, HARVESTERS & HAIRSTREAKS

Malay Gem ■ *Poritia philota* 14–16mm

DESCRIPTION Small butterfly. Male has bluish-greenish markings on uppersides of forewings. Female brown with slight orange scales on median regions of both wings, and bluish submarginal spots on uppersides of forewings. Underside brown, with several irregular, narrow brown and white line markings. **LARVAL FOODPLANTS** Currently unknown, but probably plants in Combretaceae family. **DISTRIBUTION** Subspecies *glennuydai* occurs in Central and West Luzon; subspecies *mindora* in Mindoro; subspecies *phare* in Basilan, Bohol, Dinagat, Leyte, Marinduque, Mindanao, Negros, Panaon and Samar. **HABITATS** Has only been seen in forested habitats.

Montana Bluejohn ■ *Deramas montana* 15–17mm

DESCRIPTION Small brown butterfly with metallic blue-green streaks on both wings (larger on hindwing). Female unknown. Underside brown with pale, irregular brown lines. **LARVAL FOODPLANTS** Currently unknown. **DISTRIBUTION** Occurs on Mt Kitanglad in north Mindanao. **HABITATS** Flies in forested habitats.

White Darkie ■ *Allotinus fallax* 17mm

DESCRIPTION Small butterfly with narrow wings. Upperside of male brown with white patch. Female looks similar, but has more pronounced and larger white patch. Smear-like white patch on hindwing of female. Both sexes have same underside, with brown and white speckled markings. **LARVAL FOODPLANTS** Caterpillars have been found on *Chromolaena odorata* (Asteraceae family), and were tended by ants. **DISTRIBUTION** Subspecies *fallax* occurs in Bohol, Cebu, Leyte, Luzon, Marinduque, Masbate, Panay, Samar

and Sibuyan; subspecies *aphacus* in Caminguin de Mindanao, Dinagat, Homonhon, Mindanao and Panaon; subspecies *eryximachus* in Mindoro; subspecies *dotion* in Basilan; subspecies *tymphrestus* in Jolo, Sibutu and Tawi Tawi; subspecies *negrosensis* in Negros. **HABITATS** In Negros, flies in forested habitats and also in cleared areas.

Blue Darkie ■ *Allotinus subviolaceus* 14mm

DESCRIPTION Small butterfly similar to White Darkie (above), but upperside white markings oblong shaped and have distinct bluish composition. **LARVAL FOODPLANTS**

Currently unknown, but may be similar to those of other species; also tended by ants. **DISTRIBUTION** Subspecies *subviolaceus* occurs in Balabac, Calamian, Leyte, Luzon, Mindoro, Mindanao, Palawan, Sibuyan and Sibutu. **HABITATS** Has been seen in forested areas of Palawan.

Pale Mottle

■ *Logania marmorata* 11–13mm

DESCRIPTION Small butterfly. Male brown with dusty white patch on forewing, originating from base and spreading towards median region. Female similar. Underside brown with distinct markings. **LARVAL HOSTS** Currently unknown, but caterpillar documented feeding on aphids. **DISTRIBUTION** Subspecies *palawana* occurs in Balabac, Calamian, Luzon, Marinduque and Palawan; subspecies *faustina* in Jolo, Leyte, Mindanao, Samar and Tawi Tawi; subspecies *hilaeira* in Mapun; subspecies *samosata* in Cebu, Mindoro and Negros. **HABITATS** Flies in forested areas.

Great Brownie

■ *Miletus symethus* 20mm

DESCRIPTION Small brown butterfly with narrow wings. Male brown with greyish-white patch near base, and spreading towards median section of upperside of forewings. Female similar but has whiter markings. Underside brown with curving median white band on forewings; hindwing brown with inconspicuous short, dark brown bands. **LARVAL HOSTS** Currently unknown, but caterpillar probably utilizes aphids, like other species in genus. **DISTRIBUTION** Subspecies *edonus* occurs in Palawan; subspecies *hierophantes* in Basilan, Jolo, Mindanao and Tawi Tawi; subspecies *phantus* in Luzon, Marinduque, Negros and Panay; subspecies *philopator* in Mindoro. **HABITATS** Flies in forested areas, and can be seen perching on shrubs along forest trails and forest edges.

Philippine Brownie
▪ *Miletus melanion* 19–20mm

DESCRIPTION Small butterfly. Male dark brown with conspicuous white brand on vein 4 of forewing. White patch on tornal region. Female similar, but with more rounded wings. Forewing has white patch positioned centrally and near tornal region. Underside brown with narrow, winding band on apex of forewing, and circular or oblong brown spot at tornus. **LARVAL HOSTS** Currently unknown, but caterpillars have been documented feeding on aphids. **DISTRIBUTION** Subspecies *melanion* occurs in Batanes, Balut, Luzon, Marinduque, Mindanao, Negros and Palawan; subspecies *euphranor* in Leyte and Mindoro. **HABITATS** Flies in forested areas, and can be seen perching on shrubs along forest trails and forest edges.

Apefly ▪ *Spalgis epius* 10–13mm

DESCRIPTION Small butterfly. Male dark brown with pointy forewing. Female looks similar but has more rounded forewing, and white cell-end spot is visible. Underside pale brown, with several irregular black lines throughout wings. **LARVAL HOSTS** Caterpillars feed on certain species of scale insect, on *Glycine* (Leguminosae) and *Streblus* (Moraceae). **DISTRIBUTION** Subspecies *strigatus* occurs in Bohol, Cebu, Homonhon, Leyte, Luzon, Marinduque, Masbate, Mindoro, Mindanao, Negros, Palawan, Panay, Sanga Sanga, Sibuyan, Siquijor, Sibutu, Tawi Tawi and Ticao. **HABITATS** Flies mostly in forested areas, and can be seen flying briefly at tree-tops, before perching again on a leaf.

Sunbeam ▪ *Curetis tagalica* 17–20mm

DESCRIPTION Small butterfly. Upperside forewing of male bright orange, with dark margins broadening on apex. Underside of male silver, dusted with median irregular band. Female dark brown with orange patches on both wings. **LARVAL FOODPLANTS** Certain plant species (possibly *Pongamia*) in Fabaceae family. **DISTRIBUTION** Subspecies *tagalica* occurs throughout the Philippines, except in Balabac, Dumaran, Palawan and Sibutu; subspecies *palawanica* in Balabac, Dumaran and Palawan; subspecies *takanamii* in Sibutu. **HABITATS** In Negros, seen flying at tree-tops, occasionally perching on shrubs, then flying again at tree-tops, flashing its orange colouration.

Common Ciliate Blue
▪ *Anthene emolus* 12–16mm

DESCRIPTION Small butterfly. Upperside of male metallic purple. Female brown with metallic blue/purple marking originating at bases of wings and spreading towards mid-section. Undersides of both sexes brown with distinct positioning of white bars. **LARVAL FOODPLANTS** Currently unknown, but probably plants in Anacardiaceae, Sapindaceae, Meliaceae and Combretaceae families. **DISTRIBUTION** Occurs in Balabac, Calamian, Luzon, Palawan and Tawi Tawi. **HABITATS** Flies in various habitats, including forests and home gardens. Flies with some *Jamides* species.

Pointed Ciliate Blue ■ *Anthene lycaenina* 13–15mm

DESCRIPTION Small butterfly that looks similar to Common Ciliate Blue (p. 95), but has whiter parallel lines on underside. **LARVAL FOODPLANTS** Currently unknown, but probably plants in Anacardiaceae, Sapindaceae, Meliaceae and Combretaceae families. **DISTRIBUTION** Subspecies *villosina* occurs in Balabac, Cebu, Dumaran, Leyte, Luzon, Mindoro, Mindanao, Palawan, Negros, Panay and Tawi Tawi. **HABITATS** Flies in forested habitats, and can be seen at forest edges and on forest trails, nectaring on flowering plants.

Transparent Six-Lineblue
■ *Nacaduba kurava* 13–15mm

DESCRIPTION Small butterfly. Male upperside metallic purple; female metallic pale blue with broad wing margins (costa towards tornus). Underside has similar pattern to those of other *Nacaduba* species. **LARVAL FOODPLANTS** Currently unknown, but probably *Vateria* (Dipterocarpaceae family). **DISTRIBUTION** Subspecies *kurava* occurs in Basilan, Calamian, Cebu, Dinagat, Leyte, Luzon, Marinduque, Masbate, Mindoro, Mindanao, Negros, Palawan, Panay, Samar and Sibuyan. **HABITATS** Flies in forested habitats, and can be seen along forest edges.

Common Lineblue
▪ *Prosotas nora* 10–12mm

DESCRIPTION Small butterfly. Male upperside purple-blue. Tailed species; three lines on underside of forewing at more or less the same distance. Female not illustrated in literature, but brown with blue patch. **LARVAL FOODPLANTS** Various plants such as *Acacia* species (Fabaceae), *Mallotus philippensis* (Euphorbiaceae) and *Pithecellobium dulce* (Fabaceae). **DISTRIBUTION** Subspecies *semperi* occurs in Basilan, Cebu, Leyte, Luzon, Marinduque, Mindoro, Mindanao, Negros, Palawan, Panay and Samar. **HABITATS** Flies in various habitats, and can be seen in home gardens and along forest edges.

Tailless Lineblue ▪ *Prosotas dubiosa* 10–11mm

DESCRIPTION Small, dark brown butterfly with bluish-purple sheen. Looks similar to Common Lineblue (above), but has paler (pale brown) underside. **LARVAL FOODPLANTS** *Acacia* species (Fabaceae family), including *Pithecellobium dulce*. **DISTRIBUTION** Subspecies *subardates* occurs in Balabac, Cebu, Camiguin de Mindanao, Luzon, Marinduque, Mindoro, Mindanao, Negros, Palawan, Samar, Sibuyan and Tawi Tawi. **HABITATS** Abundant and common in urban areas and on cultivated land. Can also be seen in recently cleared areas in forests and along grassy riverbanks.

Pointed Lineblue ■ *Ionolyce helicon* 11–13mm

DESCRIPTION Small butterfly. Upperside of male purple, while female is pale black with pale bluish scales. Underside brown (reddish-brown in female), with markings distinct to this species, especially arrangement of white bars near apex of forewing. **LARVAL FOODPLANTS** Currently unknown. **DISTRIBUTION** Subspecies *merguiana* occurs in Camiguin de Luzon, Luzon, Mindoro, Mindanao, Palawan and Samar. **HABITATS** Has mostly been seen along forest edges and forest trails, and may also fly towards nearby gardens.

Straight Pierrot ■ *Caleta roxus* 13mm

DESCRIPTION Small butterfly. Male and female both black with continuous white band on upperside on both wings, terminating halfway towards median section of forewing.

Underside white with black band near bases of both wings, and some irregular-shaped black markings near margins of wings. **LARVAL FOODPLANTS** Currently unknown, but probably *Zizyphus* (Rhamnaceae family). **DISTRIBUTION** Subspecies *angustior* occurs in Bongao, Calamian, Cebu, Camiguin de Mindanao, Dinagat, Luzon, Marinduque, Masbate, Mindoro, Mindanao, Palawan, Panay, Sanga Sanga, Sibutu and Tawi Tawi. **HABITATS** Flies in forested habitats, and can be seen nectaring on flowering plants along forest edges; also found along riverbanks.

Common Cerulean ■ *Jamides celeno* 15–17mm

DESCRIPTION Small butterfly. Both sexes have pale blue scales on uppersides; female has broader black margins broadening on apex of forewing. Fourth (starting near base) white band on underside forewing straight. **LARVAL FOODPLANTS** Needs further verification, but caterpillar probably feeds on *Pongamia* species (Fabaceae family). In other countries, feeds on *Saraca* and *Trichilia*. **DISTRIBUTION** Subspecies *lydanus* occurs throughout the Philippines. **HABITATS** Common in primary and secondary forests, and can be seen, rarely, in coastal areas.

Burmese Cerulean ■ *Jamides philatus* 14–17mm

DESCRIPTION Small butterfly. Male shiny blue with visible irregular white lines and markings. Female paler, with broader black margins broadening on apex, and submarginal black spot on hindwing conspicuous. Undersides of both sexes have darker submarginal markings or spots. **LARVAL FOODPLANTS** Currently unknown, but probably plants in Fabaceae family. **DISTRIBUTION** Subspecies *osias* occurs in Basilan, Jolo, Leyte, Luzon, Marinduque, Masbate, Mindoro, Negros, Palawan, Panay, Sibuyan, Siquijor, Sibutu, Tawi Tawi and Ticao. **HABITATS** Has been seen in a forested habitat, and may also fly in coastal areas.

Aratus Cerulean
▪ *Jamides aratus* 13–17mm

DESCRIPTION Small butterfly. Both sexes very pale, but female has broad black margins on forewings. Conspicuous black spots (circular and triangular) on submarginal regions of hindwings. **LARVAL FOODPLANTS** Currently unknown, but probably plants in Fabaceae family. **DISTRIBUTION** Subspecies *adana* occurs in Balabac, Calamian, Palawan, Sibutu and Tawi Tawi. **HABITATS** Has been seen in forested areas of Palawan.

Metallic Cerulean ▪ *Jamides alecto* 20–21mm

DESCRIPTION Small butterfly. Bright metallic blue upperside. Grey on underside with white banding. Black-centred, orange-crowned eye-spot on tornal area of hindwing. Some additional submarginal orange markings. **LARVAL FOODPLANTS** Certain ginger (Zingiberaceae) and legume (Fabaceae) plants, possibly including *Pongamia* species. **DISTRIBUTION** Subspecies *manilana* occurs in Catanduanes, Cebu, Dinagat, Leyte, Luzon, Marinduque, Masbate, Mindoro, Mindanao, Negros, Panay and Samar; subspecies *kawazoie* in Balabac and Palawan. **HABITATS** Common and abundant in primary and secondary forests, and may also fly in coastal areas where its host plant is found.

Dark Cerulean ■ *Jamides bochus* 16–17mm

DESCRIPTION Small butterfly. Upperside of male metallic purple with black wing margins. Female similar but with purple markings. Underside pale brown with paler white (slightly broader in female) parallel markings. **LARVAL FOODPLANTS** Certain ginger (Zingiberaceae) and legume (Fabaceae) plants, possibly including *Pongamia*, *Derris*, *Crotalaria* and *Phaseolus*. **DISTRIBUTION** Subspecies *bochus* occurs in Balabac, Bongao, Calamian, Palawan, Sanga Sanga, Sibutu and Tawi Tawi; subspecies *pulchrior* in Batanes, Bohol, Catanduanes, Cebu, Dinagat, Leyte, Luzon, Marinduque, Masbate, Mindoro, Mindanao, Negros, Panaon, Panay, Samar and Sibuyan. **HABITATS** Has been seen in primary forests.

White Cerulean

■ *Jamides pura* 11–18mm

DESCRIPTION Small, silvery-white butterfly. Female has very broad black marginal band. Underside pale brown with long white parallel lines and conspicuous orange patch near tail. **LARVAL FOODPLANTS** Certain ginger (Zingiberaceae) and legume (Fabaceae) plants. **DISTRIBUTION** Subspecies *eordaea* occurs in Balabac and Palawan. **HABITATS** Has been seen in forested areas of Palawan.

Silver Forget-me-not ▪ *Catochrysops panormus* 13–16mm

DESCRIPTION Small butterfly. Male metallic pale blue. Female dark brown with bluish dusting near bases of both wings spreading towards middle sections. Underside pale brown with distinct markings such as white bars and two black spots on costa of hindwings. Recognized by tiny black spot on costa of forewing positioned near white bars close to

wing margins. **LARVAL FOODPLANTS** Fabaceae family plants, such as *Pongamia, Butea, Acacia* and *Desmodium*. **DISTRIBUTION** Subspecies *exiguus* occurs in Balabac, Cebu, Dinagat, Masbate, Mindanao, Negros, Palawan, Sarangani, Sibutu and Tawi Tawi. **HABITATS** Flies in various habitats, including forests, cultivated land and home gardens.

Forget-me-not ▪ *Catochrysops strabo* 13–16mm

DESCRIPTION Small butterfly. Male metallic pale purple, while female looks similar to Silver Forget-me-not (above). Underside also similar, but tiny black spot on costa of Forget-me-not is positioned between the two white bars. **LARVAL FOODPLANTS** Fabaceae family plants, such as *Pongamia, Butea, Acacia* and *Desmodium*. **DISTRIBUTION** Subspecies *luzonensis* occurs in Balabac, Basilan, Bohol, Cebu, Camiguin de Mindanao, Dinagat, Dumaran, Jolo, Leyte, Luzon, Masbate, Mindoro, Mindanao, Palawan, Panay, Samar, Sarangani and Sibuyan. **HABITATS** Flies in various habitats, including forests, cultivated land and home gardens.

Pea Blue ▪ *Lampides boeticus* 14–18mm

DESCRIPTION Small butterfly. Male bluish-purple; female brown with bluish dusting on basal region. Brown underside with similar patterns to *Jamides* species, but very distinct to this species. Black spots with orange scales on top of tornal region of underside hindwings. **LARVAL FOODPLANTS** Mostly various plants in Fabaceae family, including *Cajanus, Caesalpinia, Crotalaria, Butea, Vigna, Pisum* and *Pongamia*. **DISTRIBUTION** Found throughout the Philippines. **HABITATS** Abundant in disturbed areas, and can be seen in home gardens, roadsides and forest edges.

Zebra Blue ▪ *Leptotes plinius* 16mm

DESCRIPTION Small butterfly known for 'zebra' markings on underside. Male blue; female white with blue dusting on basal region. 'Zebra' markings visible from upperside, and two conspicuous black spots enveloped with orange and silvery-yellow on tornal region of hindwings. **LARVAL FOODPLANTS** *Plumbago, Albizia* and *Mimosa*. **DISTRIBUTION** Subspecies *leopardus* occurs in Leyte, Luzon, Mindanao (Surigao and south Cotabato), and Negros. **HABITATS** Flies in forested habitats, and can be seen in nearby gardens or along forest edges. May also prefer shaded habitats.

Common Pierrot

■ *Castalius rosimon* 14mm

DESCRIPTION Small white butterfly with broad black margins on both wings. Black-bluish dusting near bases of both wings. Underside white with less pronounced black margins; most of irregular-shaped black markings on upperside visible on underside. **LARVAL FOODPLANTS** Currently unknown, but probably *Ziyphus* and *Paliurus* (Rhamnaceae family). **DISTRIBUTION** Subspecies *monrosi* occurs in Luzon and Samar. **HABITATS** Flies in forested habitats.

Dark Grass Blue

■ *Zizeeria karsandra* 10–11mm

DESCRIPTION Small butterfly. Male bluish and female dark brown. Conspicuous cell spot on underside of forewing. **LARVAL FOODPLANTS** *Amaranthus* species (Amaranthaceae family) and plants in Fabaceae family. **DISTRIBUTION** Occurs in Cebu, Jolo, Luzon, Marinduque, Mindanao, Negros and Palawan. **HABITATS** Common and abundant in disturbed habitats, and can be seen flying at ground level along roadsides and in home gardens. Flies with Lesser and Tiny Grass Blues (opposite).

Lesser Grass Blue ■ *Zizina otis* 10–12mm

DESCRIPTION Small butterfly. Male and female bluish, but female darker. No cell spot on underside of forewing. **LARVAL FOODPLANTS** Various plants, such as *Amaranthus*, *Desmodium*, *Sesbania* and *Alysicarpus*. **DISTRIBUTION** Subspecies *oriens* occurs in Bohol, Cebu, Dinagat, Dumaran, Jolo, Leyte, Luzon, Marinduque, Mindoro, Mindanao, Negros, Palawan and Sarangani. **HABITATS** Common and abundant in disturbed and grassy habitats, and can also be seen flying at ground level along roadsides, and in home gardens and ball fields. Flies with Dark and Tiny Grass Blues (opposite and below).

Tiny Grass Blue ■ *Zizula hylax* 8–10mm

DESCRIPTION Smaller than Dark Grass and Lesser Grass Blues (opposite and above). Lacks cell spot, but has several spots reaching costa and above cell on underside of forewing. **LARVAL FOODPLANTS** *Lantana camara* and *Ruellia* species. **DISTRIBUTION** Subspecies *pygmaea* occurs in Cebu, Leyte, Luzon, Marinduque, Negros, Palawan, Sibutu and Tawi Tawi. **HABITATS** Common and abundant butterfly that can be seen in disturbed habitats, roadsides, home gardens and ball fields.

Forest Quaker
■ *Pithecops corvus* 12–13mm

DESCRIPTION Small, dark brown to black butterfly. Underside silvery-white with large, circular black spot on apex of hindwing. **LARVAL FOODPLANTS** Currently unknown, but probably *Desmodium* (Fabaceae) and *Gardenia* (Rubiaceae). **DISTRIBUTION** Subspecies *corax* occurs in Basilan, Bohol, Leyte, Luzon, Marinduque, Masbate, Mindoro, Mindanao, Palawan, Panay, Panaon, Samar, Sanga Sanga and Sibutu. **HABITATS** Flies in forested habitats and can be seen along forest trails and in forest edges.

Common Quaker ■ *Neopithecops zalmora* 9–12mm

DESCRIPTION Small, dark brown butterfly with faded white spot on median of forewing. Underside white with conspicuous circular black spot on costa apex of hindwing. **LARVAL FOODPLANTS** *Glycosmis* (Rutaceae family). **DISTRIBUTION** Subspecies *zalmora* occurs in Cebu, Leyte, Luzon, Mindanao, Palawan and Tawi Tawi. **HABITATS** Flies in forested habitats, and can be seen along riverbanks or in shaded places.

Malayan

■ *Megisba malaya* 10–13mm

DESCRIPTION Small butterfly. Male and female dark brown with conspicuous faded white narrow patch in middle of forewings. Underside white with black markings distinct to this species, especially tiny black markings on costa of forewing. **LARVAL FOODPLANTS** Currently unknown, but probably *Mallotus* (Euphorbiaeae) and *Rhamnus* (Rhamnaceae). **DISTRIBUTION** Subspecies *sikkima* occurs in Balabac, Bohol, Cebu, Leyte, Luzon, Marinduque, Masbate, Mindoro, Mindanao, Negros, Palawan, Panay, Samar, Sibuyan, Sibutu and Tawi Tawi. **HABITATS** Flies in forested habitats, and can be seen along forest trails and forest edges.

Narrow-bordered Hedge Blue ■ *Udara placidula* 13–17mm

DESCRIPTION Small butterfly. Male dark purplish blue with black margins slightly broadening on apex. Female light brown with large white patches on both wings, and slightly blue dusted. **LARVAL FOODPLANTS** Currently unknown, but probably plants in Polygonaceae family. **DISTRIBUTION** Subspecies *placidula* occurs in north Mindoro; subspecies *kawazoei* in Leyte, Luzon, Mindanao, Negros and Palawan. **HABITATS** Found in primary and secondary forests, and can be seen along riverbanks.

Bicoloured Hedge Blue
■ *Udara selma* 11–12mm

DESCRIPTION Small butterfly. Male shiny pale blue. Female light brown with large white patch, and blue dusted. Entire hindwing of female white and blue dusted. **LARVAL FOODPLANTS** Currently unknown, but probably plants in Polygonaceae family. **DISTRIBUTION** Subspecies *arsina* occurs in Mindoro; subspecies *mindanensis* in Mindanao, Negros, Palawan and Panay. **HABITATS** Flies in primary and secondary forests, and can be seen along forest edges.

Dilectissima Hedge Blue
■ *Udara dilectissima* 12–15mm

DESCRIPTION Small butterfly. Male metallic purple with inconspicuous pale white bands on hindwing. Female white with bluish scales near wing-base and broad black on margin and costa of forewing. Underside silvery-white with black spots. Looks similar to Bicoloured Hedge Blue (above). **LARVAL FOODPLANTS** Currently unknown, but probably plants in Polygonaceae family. **DISTRIBUTION** Subspecies *luzona* occurs in Luzon, Marinduque, Mindanao and Negros. **HABITATS** Flies in primary and secondary forests.

Common Hedge Blue ▪ *Acytolepis puspa* 14–15mm

DESCRIPTION Small butterfly. Male metallic purplish-blue. Female brown with large white patches and blue dusting proximally. Spot on space 2 of forewing underside positioned inwardly or not aligned with spots on spaces 3–5. **LARVAL FOODPLANTS** Various plants such as *Shorea* (Dipterocarpaceae), *Cratoxylum* (Hypericaceae), *Bridelia* (Euphorbiaceae), *Schleichera* (Sapindaceae), *Hiptage* (Malpighiaceae), *Xylia* (Mimosaceae), *Glochidion* (Phyllanthaceae) and *Myrica* (Myricaceae). **DISTRIBUTION** Subspecies *cagaya* occurs in Luzon, Marinduque, Masbate, Mindoro, Palawan, Panay, Polillo and Sibuyan; subspecies *bazilana* in Basilan, Cebu, Camiguin de Mindanao, Dinagat, Jolo, Leyte, Mindanao, Samar and Tawi Tawi. **HABITATS** Flies in primary and secondary forests.

Southern Hedge Blue ▪ *Celarchus archagathos* 15mm

DESCRIPTION Small butterfly. One-third of the male's wing black distally, and blue to white dusted proximally. Male very similar to Hermarchus Hedge Blue (p. 110), but spots on submarginal region of hindwing not well pronounced. Female similar to female Hermarchus. **LARVAL FOODPLANTS** Currently unknown, but probably plants in Fabaceae, Aceraceae and Ulmaceae families. **DISTRIBUTION** Subspecies *leytensis* occurs in south Leyte; subspecies *archagathos* in Basilan, Camiguin de Mindanao and Mindanao. **HABITATS** Flies in primary and secondary forests.

Hermarchus Hedge Blue
■ *Celarchus hermarchus* 15mm

DESCRIPTION Small butterfly. Submarginal spots well pronounced in both sexes. Male silvery-blue with large white circular patches on both wings. Female brown with large white patches, and blue dusted proximally. **LARVAL FOODPLANTS** Currently unknown, but probably plants in Fabaceae, Aceraceae and Ulmaceae families. **DISTRIBUTION** Subspecies *hermarchus* occurs in Luzon, Marinduque, Masbate, Negros and Panay; subspecies *vesontia* in Mindoro, Romblon, Samar and Sibuyan. **HABITATS** Flies in primary and secondary forests.

Philippine Hedge Blue ■ *Celastrina philippina* 12–13mm

DESCRIPTION Small butterfly. Male metallic purplish-blue with submarginal spots on hindwing. Female dark brown to black with large white patches; blue dusting basally, spreading to middle part of wings. **LARVAL FOODPLANTS** Currently unknown, but probably plants in Fabaceae, Aceraceae and Ulmaceae families. **DISTRIBUTION** Subspecies *philippina* occurs in Camotes, Luzon, Masbate, Mindanao, Negros and Palawan. **HABITATS** Flies in moist habitats and along riverbanks in forested areas. May fly with other *Celastrina* species.

Gram Blue ■ *Euchrysops cnejus* 12–16mm

DESCRIPTION Small butterfly. Male purple-blue with black spots (with orange scales on top) on spaces 1b and 2 on hindwings. Female brown and blue dusted proximally. Underside pale brown with conspicuous black spots enveloped in orange scales, and yellow-green dusting on spaces 1b and 2 of hindwing. Yellow-green dusting obsolete in some populations. **LARVAL FOODPLANTS** Mostly plants in Fabaceae family, such as *Acacia*, *Vigna*, *Butea* and *Canavalia*.

DISTRIBUTION Subspecies *cnejus* occurs in Balabac, Cebu, Dinagat, Leyte, Luzon, Marinduque, Mindoro, Mindanao, Negros, Palawan, Sarangani and Tawi Tawi.

HABITATS Common in disturbed habitats, and can also be seen along roadsides and in home gardens.

Lime Blue ■ *Chilades lajus* 8mm

DESCRIPTION Small butterfly. Upperside of male blue. Female blue but has darker wing borders. Underside has series of white-enveloped black spots. Spot on space 7 on hindwing larger and darker, and aligned with spot on space 6 (slightly positioned inwards); spot on space 4 oblong shaped. **LARVAL FOODPLANTS** *Citrus*, *Severinia*, *Triphasia*, *Limonia* and *Atalantia*. Caterpillars also known to feed on aphids. **DISTRIBUTION** Subspecies *athena* occurs in Bohol, Camiguin de Luzon, Dinagat, Homonhon, Leyte, Luzon, Marinduque, Mindanao, Palawan, Panay, Samar, Sarangani, Sanga Sanga, Sibuyan and Tawi Tawi. **HABITATS** Flies in various habitats.

Mindoro Cupid
■ *Chilades mindora* 15–18mm

DESCRIPTION Small butterfly. Male purple. Female darker, with blue scaling proximally. Tornal area of hindwing has conspicuous orange scales enveloping black spots. Underside cream-white with black markings more pronounced. Hindwing tornal spots enveloped by orange scales. **LARVAL FOODPLANTS** Cycadaceae family; probably feeds on plants similar to Lime Blue (p. 111). **DISTRIBUTION** Found in Bongao, Calamian, Cebu, Camiguin de Luzon, Homonhon, Leyte, Luzon, Marinduque, Masbate, Mindoro, Mindanao, Negros, Palawan, Samar, Sanga Sanga, Tawi Tawi and Ticao. **HABITATS** Flies in various habitats, and can be seen flying near its host plant. In Negros mostly recorded near cycads/cycas along coastal areas.

Plains Cupid ■ *Chilades pandava* 15mm

DESCRIPTION Small butterfly. Male has metallic purple upperside, while female is dark brown with slightly bluish scales. Underside pale brown with black and dark brown markings distinct for this genus. **LARVAL FOODPLANTS** Cycads/cycas (Cycadaceae family). **DISTRIBUTION** Subspecies *vapanda* occurs in Leyte and Luzon. **HABITATS** Flies near host plant, and may fly in various habitats.

Small Grass Jewel
■ *Freyeria putli* 10mm

DESCRIPTION Very small butterfly that looks like *Zizina*, *Zizeeria* and *Zizula* species. Dark grey with five very conspicuous black spots; orange scaling lined up along submarginal region of hindwing underside. **LARVAL FOODPLANTS** *Heliotropium* (Boraginaceae), and *Alysicarpus*, *Flemingia*, *Indigofera*, *Lotus*, *Pisum*, *Rhynchosia* and *Zornia* (Fabaceae). Caterpillars attended by ants. **DISTRIBUTION** Subspecies *gnoma* occurs in Cebu, Luzon, Negros, Siquijor and Mindanao. Recorded on other islands. **HABITATS** Flies near host plants in coastal areas.

Peacock Oakblue ■ *Arhopala horsfieldi* 20–23mm

DESCRIPTION Medium-sized butterfly. Upperside of male brown with distinct metallic green patch (extending only halfway along forewing and smaller on hindwing). Female has metallic purple patch. Underside brown with distinct arrangements of dark brown bars. **LARVAL FOODPLANTS** Currently unknown, but probably plants in Fagaceae (*Lithocarpus*), Myrtaceae, Combretaceae, Loranthaceae, Fabaceae, Sapindaceae and Dipterocarpaceae families. **DISTRIBUTION** Subspecies *palawanica* occurs in Palawan. **HABITATS** Flies in forested habitats.

Magnificent Oakblue ▪ *Arhopala anthelus* 26–29mm

DESCRIPTION Small butterfly. Male metallic sky-blue, while female can vary from brown to metallic sky-blue, with very broad black wing margins. Underside brown with pastel purple-pink. Cell on forewing has three large spots, and there are spots below costa. Space 8 on hindwing has two spots, and space 6 has incomplete spot (half only). **LARVAL FOODPLANTS** Currently unknown, but probably plants in Fagaceae and Euphorbiaceae families. **DISTRIBUTION** Subspecies *marinduquensis* occurs in Marinduque; subspecies *sotades* in Bohol, Leyte, south Luzon, Mindanao, Panaon and Samar; subspecies *saturatior* in Palawan; subspecies *sanmariana* in Babuyan and north-east Luzon; subspecies *reverie* in Negros and Panay; subspecies *paradisii* in Dinagat; subspecies *impar* in Mindoro. **HABITATS** Flies in primary and secondary forests.

Corbet Dull Oakblue

▪ *Arhopala agesilaus* 20mm

DESCRIPTION Small butterfly. Male dark metallic purple with broad dark wing margins. Female looks similar but has less purple metallic scaling (more pronounced on forewing). Spot on space 6 of hindwing wider and closer to spot on space 5 than to cell-end spot. **LARVAL FOODPLANTS** Currently unknown, but probably plants in Fagaceae and Euphorbiaceae families. **DISTRIBUTION** Subspecies *philippa* occurs in Bohol, Dinagat, Leyte, Luzon, Mindoro, Mindanao, Negros, Polillo and Samar; subspecies *agesilaus* in Palawan. **HABITATS** Flies in primary and secondary forests.

Hesba Oakblue
■ *Arhopala hesba* 20–25mm

DESCRIPTION Small butterfly. Male metallic sky-blue. Female looks similar but has darker and broader wing margins. Underside dark brown (spots darker), with reddish-pinkish-purple composition. Forewing spots io spaces 5 and 6 positioned outwardly. Triangular or irregular spot at start of veins 2 and 3. **LARVAL FOODPLANTS** Currently unknown, but probably plants in Fagaceae and Euphorbiaceae families. **DISTRIBUTION** Found in Bohol, Leyte, Mindoro, Mindanao, Negros and Samar. **HABITATS** Flies in primary and secondary forests.

Aberrant Oakblue ■ *Arhopala abseus* 12–17mm

DESCRIPTION Small butterfly. Male metallic purple with broad dark wing margins. Female similar but blue instead of purple. Underside dark brown, with some pink-purple composition with darker markings and spots. Post-discal spots on forewing fused, forming irregular band. Very light brown patch on costa of hindwing can be present. **LARVAL FOODPLANTS** *Shorea* (Dipterocarpaceae family), and possibly plants in Fagaceae family. **DISTRIBUTION** Subspecies *abseus* occurs in Balabac, Calamian and Palawan; subspecies *amphea* in Bohol, Camiguin de Luzon, Dinagat, Leyte, Luzon, Marinduque, Mindoro, Mindanao, Negros, Panay, Panaon, Samar and Sibuyan. **HABITATS** Flies in primary and secondary forests; can also be seen along forest edges and forest trails.

Lined Oakblue
■ *Arhopala aronya* 13–17mm

DESCRIPTION Small butterfly. Male metallic blue, while female is paler with dark, broader wing margins on both wings. Underside dark brown with much broader white lines forming maze. **LARVAL FOODPLANTS** Currently unknown, but probably plants in Fagaceae and Euphorbiaceae families. **DISTRIBUTION** Subspecies *aronya* occurs in Dinagat, Leyte and Mindanao; subspecies *mangyan* in Mindoro; subspecies *natsumiae* in Negros; subspecies *kalinga* in Luzon and Marinduque. **HABITATS** Flies in primary and secondary forests.

Purple Broken-band Oakblue ■ *Arhopala alitaeus* 16–17mm

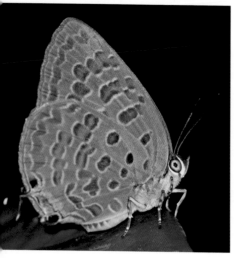

DESCRIPTION Small butterfly. Male metallic blue with narrow black margins on forewing; slightly broader on hindwing. Female dark brown with metallic blue patch on median part of forewing. Forewing spot on space 4 positioned outwardly, and spot on space 6 of hindwing very wide, overlapping with cell-end spot and spot on space 5. **LARVAL FOODPLANTS** Currently unknown, but probably plants in Fagaceae and Euphorbiaceae families. **DISTRIBUTION** Subspecies *panta* occurs in Leyte, Mindanao, Panaon and Samar; subspecies *masarana* in Calayan and Camiguin de Luzon; subspecies *myrtale* in Calamian and Palawan; subspecies *magellanus* in Homonhon; subspecies *zilensis* in Basilan. **HABITATS** Flies in primary and secondary forests.

Shigae Oakblue ▪ *Arhopala shigae* 20mm

DESCRIPTION Small butterfly. Once a subspecies of Purple Broken-band Oakblue (opposite). Male looks similar to this species, but has narrower black wing margins. Female also similar, but has larger metallic blue patch on forewing. In some individuals entire hindwing heavily white dusted, so spots and markings are almost completely covered. Forewing spots on spaces 4 and 6 positioned slightly outwardly. **LARVAL FOODPLANTS** Currently unknown, but probably plants in Myrtaceae, Combretaceae, Loranthaceae, Fabaceae, Sapindaceae and Dipterocarpaceae families. **DISTRIBUTION** Found in Bohol, Cebu, Luzon, Marinduque, Masbate, Negros, Panay and Sibuyan. **HABITATS** Flies in forested areas, and can also be seen nectaring in neighbouring home gardens.

Centaur Oakblue ▪ *Arhopala centaurus* 20–25mm

DESCRIPTION Small butterfly. Both sexes metallic purple-blue, but female has broader margins, especially on forewing. Two forewing cell spots near base, and central spots conspicuously 'U' shaped. Underside dark brown with reddish composition. **LARVAL FOODPLANTS** Currently unknown, but probably various plants such as *Syzygium* (Myrtaceae), *Terminalia* (Combretaceae), and other species in Loranthaceae, Fabaceae, Sapindaceae and Dipterocarpaceae families. **DISTRIBUTION** Subspecies *aglais* occurs in Leyte, Lubang, Luzon, Marinduque, Masbate, Mindoro, Mindanao, Polillo, Samar, Sibuyan and Tawi Tawi; subspecies *nakula* in Calamian, Dumaran, Lanapacan and Palawan; subspecies *cuyoensis* in Cuyo; subspecies *decimarie* in Homonhon; subspecies *dinacola* in Dinagat; subspecies *babuyana* in Batanes and Camiguin de Luzon. **HABITATS** Flies in various habitats, and mostly encountered in forested areas. Also visits neighbouring home gardens.

Bifid Plushblue
■ *Flos diardi* 21mm

DESCRIPTION Small butterfly. Male metallic purple blue. Female paler, with broader wing margins. Underside has very conspicuous 'thumbs-up' marking on cell of forewing. Markings distinct and clearly outlined. **LARVAL FOODPLANTS** Currently unknown, but probably plants in Myrtaceae, Combretaceae and Fagaceae families. **DISTRIBUTION** Subspecies *capeta* occurs in Bohol, Leyte, Luzon, Marinduque, Masbate, Mindoro, Mindanao, Negros, Palawan, Panaon, Polillo, Samar, Sanga Sanga, Sibutu and Tawi Tawi. **HABITATS** Flies in primary and secondary forests, and can be seen flying and perching on tree-tops.

Plain Plushblue ■ *Flos apidanus* 20–22mm

DESCRIPTION Small butterfly. Male purple. Female sky-blue with broad brown wing margins. Underside has very conspicuous, outlined, 'heart-shaped' marking. Body at centre

of heart-shaped marking. **LARVAL FOODPLANTS** Currently unknown, but probably plants in Myrtaceae and Combretaceae families. **DISTRIBUTION** Subspecies *himna* occurs in Mindanao; subspecies *palawanus* in Balabac, Bohol, Calamian, Cebu, Camiguin de Mindanao, Luzon, Marinduque, Mindoro, Palawan, Panay and Samar; subspecies *saturatus* in Sibutu and Tawi Tawi. **HABITATS** Flies in primary and secondary forests, and can be seen flying and perching on tree-tops.

Philippine Acacia Blue
▪ *Surendra manilana* 15–16mm

DESCRIPTION Small butterfly.
Male metallic blue; female looks
similar. Conspicuous, irregular brown
line on median of forewing that
continues on hindwing. **LARVAL
FOODPLANTS** Currently unknown,
but in other countries caterpillar feeds
on plants in Fabaceae family, which
includes *Albizia*, *Saraca* and *Mimosa*.
DISTRIBUTION Subspecies *manilana*
occurs in Leyte, Luzon, Marinduque,
Mindoro, Mindanao, Negros, Panay,
Samar and Sibuyan; subspecies
johnelioti in Bongao. **HABITATS** Flies
in primary and secondary forests.

Leaf Blue ▪ *Amblypodia narada* 25–28mm

DESCRIPTION Medium-sized butterfly. Male ranges from metallic purple to blue with
dark wing margins broadening at apex. Female light brown with purple-dusted patches.

Underside brown with not
many detailed markings,
apart from dark median
line originating from apex
of forewing to anal region
of hindwing. **LARVAL
FOODPLANTS** Currently
unknown, but probably
Syzygium (Myrtaceae) and *Olax*
(Olacaceae). **DISTRIBUTION**
Subspecies *erichsonii* occurs
in Cebu, Camiguin de Luzon,
Luzon, Marinduque, Mindoro,
Negros, Palawan and Panay;
subspecies *sibutuensis* in
Sibutu; subspecies *plateni*
in Basilan, Bohol, Bongao,
Jolo, Leyte, Mindanao, Sanga
Sanga, Samar and Tawi
Tawi. **HABITATS** Mostly
encountered along forest trails.

Scarce Silverstreak Blue ■ *Iraota rochana* 18–20mm

DESCRIPTION Small butterfly. Male metallic blue-green and female brown. Two tails. Underside has markings that are unique to this genus. Forewing has white cell streak with white spot on cell end, and meteor-shaped white marking on space 4. Hindwing has conspicuous white 'kangaroo' marking. **LARVAL FOODPLANTS** Currently unknown, but

probably *Ficus* (Moraceae family), and plants in Lythraceae family. **DISTRIBUTION** Subspecies *lazarena* occurs in Babuyan, Bohol, Cebu, Dinagat, Leyte, Luzon, Marinduque, Masbate, Mindoro, Mindanao, Panaon and Samar; subspecies *austrosuluensis* in Bongao, Sanga Sanga and Tawi Tawi; subspecies *zwickorum* in Mapun; subspecies *boudanti* in Sibutu; subspecies *indalawanae* in Balabac; subspecies *garzoni* in Negros and Panay; subspecies *ottonis* in Calamian and Palawan. **HABITATS** Flies in forested habitats, and can also be seen nectaring in nearby home gardens.

Gracilis Tinsel

■ *Catapaecilma gracilis* 13–16mm

DESCRIPTION Small butterfly. Upperside of male metallic purple. Female black with sky-blue dusting near bases of both wings. Underside orange with distinct patterns and lines of black, silver and reddish markings. **LARVAL FOODPLANTS** Currently unknown, but probably plants in Rhamnaceae, Combretaceae, Lythraceae and Euphorbiaceae families. **DISTRIBUTION** Found in Bohol, Cebu, Camiguin de Luzon, Leyte, Luzon, Marinduque, Mindoro, Mindanao, Panaon and Samar. **HABITATS** Flies in forested areas, and can be seen along forest trails and forest edges. May also fly towards nearby gardens.

Philippine Vineblue ▪ *Hypothecla astyla* 15–16mm

DESCRIPTION Small butterfly. Male dull purple with white dusting and narrow dark wing margins. Female bluish and white dusted, with broader margin especially on costa of forewing. Underside light brown with 'S'-shaped marking on middle of forewing cell. Markings look similar to those of *Arhopala* species. Two conspicuous 'J'-shaped markings on tornal region of hindwing. **LARVAL FOODPLANTS** Currently unknown, but in Siquijor female has been seen flying and perching on the same vine plant along a forest edge. **DISTRIBUTION** Subspecies *astyla* occurs in Biliran, Bohol, Leyte, Luzon, Marinduque, Mindoro, Panaon, Samar and Siquijor; subspecies *cebuensis* in Cebu; subspecies *mindanaensis* in Mindanao; subspecies *palawensis* in Palawan; subspecies *tegea* in Basilan. **HABITATS** Rare. Flies in forested areas, and can be encountered singly along forest edges and forest trails.

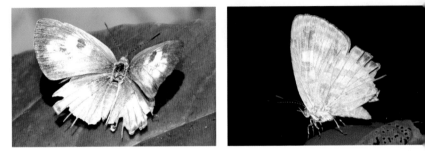

Malayan Yamfly ▪ *Loxura cassiopeia* 16–19mm

DESCRIPTION Small butterfly. Male orange with black wing margins broadening at apex. Underside yellow with inconspicuous median band formed by irregular spots. Female looks similar but has more rounded wings. **LARVAL FOODPLANTS** *Smilax* species (Smilacaceae family). **DISTRIBUTION** Subspecies *owadai* occurs in Cebu and Mindanao; subspecies *yilma* in Palawan. **HABITATS** Rare, and mostly flies in forested areas.

Branded Imperial
▪ *Eooxylides tharis* 19mm

DESCRIPTION Small butterfly. Male darker brown than female. Light brown patch near base of space 2 of forewing, and slightly pale blue dusting on tornal region proximally. Half of hindwing white with black spots. Long tail originating from vein 2. Underside dark orange on forewing and lighter on hindwing, with white thorny markings with black spots at tornal region. **LARVAL FOODPLANTS** *Smilax* species (Smilacaceae family). **DISTRIBUTION** Subspecies *tharisides* occurs in Balabac and Palawan. **HABITATS** Flies in forested habitats of Palawan.

Ambon Onyx ▪ *Horaga syrinx* 16mm

DESCRIPTION Small butterfly. Male has pale blue dusting on basal to median region. Female slightly purple dusted. Underside light brown with conspicuous pointy, large white band on forewing that continuous narrowly to median region of hindwing and curves

to anal region with green scales. **LARVAL FOODPLANTS** Caterpillar feeds on *Melicope* species (Rutaceae). **DISTRIBUTION** Subspecies *ashinica* occurs in Bohol, Camiguin de Luzon, Leyte, Luzon, Marinduque, Masbate, Mindoro, Mindanao, Negros, Panay, Panaon, Sibuyan and Siquijor; subspecies *incerta* in Bongao, Linapacan, Palawan, Sanga Sanga, Sibutu and Tawi Tawi; subspecies *camiguina* in Camiguin de Mindanao; subspecies *joloana* in Jolo; subspecies *paulla* in Basilan. **HABITATS** Rare on other islands and probably flies in various habitats, although most photographs have been taken in dense vegetation, including in forests and gardens with canopy cover.

Lefebvrei's Onyx ▪ *Horaga lefebvrei* 13–16mm

DESCRIPTION Small butterfly. Male brown with large white patch on forewing (with metallic blue scales near base) and tails on hindwing. Female similar but lacks metallic blue scales. Underside reddish-brown with large white patch occupying almost half of forewing. Unique markings on underside can vary, and white markings can be smaller or larger. **LARVAL FOODPLANTS** Caterpillar probably feeds on *Melicope* species (Rutaceae).

DISTRIBUTION Subspecies *lefebvrei* occurs in Luzon and Marinduque; subspecies *osma* in Bohol, Leyte, Mindanao, Negros, Panaon and Samar; subspecies *osmana* in Mindoro. **HABITATS** Flies mostly in forested habitats, and towards nearby gardens.

Golden-tailed Hairstreak ▪ *Cheritra orpheus* 17–22mm

DESCRIPTION Small butterfly. Male bright orange with brown streaks. Female brown-orange. Long tail originating at vein 2. Underside cream-white with orange margins. Tornal region of hindwing has black spots with green scales and irregular lines and spots. **LARVAL FOODPLANTS** Plants in Lauraceae, Fabaceae and Lythraceae families. **DISTRIBUTION** Subspecies *orpheus* occurs in Babuyan, Luzon, Marinduque, Mindoro, Negros, Panay and Ticao; subspecies *eurydice* in Calamian and Palawan; subspecies *orphnine* in Leyte, Mindanao and Samar. **HABITATS** Flies in primary and secondary forests. May also be seen nectaring in nearby parks and home gardens.

Common Posy ◼ *Drupadia ravindra* 18–19mm

DESCRIPTION Small butterfly. Male dark brown with orange circular patch positioned centrally on forewing, and blue dusting on most of hindwing. Female paler and lacks blue dusting on hindwing, but instead has pale purple-white dusting on tornal region, with at least three spots. Underside deep orange on forewing, slightly spreading towards costa of

hindwing. Base of forewing has conspicuous oblong spot and sickle-shaped marking on cell. Hindwing has several short, broad black bands scattered throughout wing. Tornal region has spots and green scales. **LARVAL FOODPLANTS** Currently unknown, but probably plants in Annonaceae, Fagaceae, Sapindaceae and Fabaceae families. **DISTRIBUTION** Subspecies *ravindrina* occurs in Calamian, Dumaran and Palawan; subspecies *resoluta* in Lubang, Luzon, Mindoro, Panay and Polillo; subspecies *okurai* in Mindanao; subspecies *joloana* in Jolo, Sanga Sanga, Sibutu and Tawi Tawi; subspecies *balabacola* in Balabac. **HABITATS** Flies in primary and secondary forests.

Pale Blue Royal ◼ *Tajuria jalajala* 16–20mm

DESCRIPTION Small butterfly. Male metallic marine-blue. Female purplish. Both sexes have black wing margins broadening at apex. Underside cream-brown and post-discal band positioned to submarginal region of forewing. Narrow black band on hindwing has broad white outer edges. **LARVAL FOODPLANTS** Currently unknown, but probably plants in Loranthaceae family (*Scurrula*). **DISTRIBUTION** Subspecies *jalajala* occurs in Biliran, Bohol, Camiguin de Luzon, Camiguin de Mindanao, Dinagat, Leyte, Luzon, Marinduque, Masbate, Mindoro, Mindanao, Negros, Panay, Panaon, Polillo and Samar; subspecies *stefii* in Homonhon. **HABITATS** Flies in forested habitats, and can be seen perching on shrubs along forest trails and forest edges.

Blue Royal ▪ *Matsutaroa iljai* 20mm

DESCRIPTION Small butterfly. Upperside of male metallic greenish-blue, with black borders occupying almost half of forewing. Female similar but paler, and wings relatively wider. Underside of male whitish-green, with conspicuous black spots near tails. Female pale brown with distinct white bars near borders of both wings. **LARVAL FOODPLANTS** Currently unknown. **DISTRIBUTION** Found in Masbate, Negros and west Panay. **HABITATS** Flies in forested areas, and can be seen nectaring on flowering plants along forest trails and forest edges.

Negros Royal ▪ *Dacalana liaoi* 17–22mm

DESCRIPTION Small butterfly with metallic greenish-blue markings on uppersides of both wings, and broad black (narrower in females) markings occupying half of forewings. Underside pale brown with conspicuous white band (tapering on hindwing) on both wings, and pair of tails on hindwing. **LARVAL FOODPLANTS** Currently unknown, but probably plants in Loranthaceae family. **DISTRIBUTION** Found in Negros and Panay. **HABITATS** Flies in forested areas, and visits nearby home gardens; rarely spotted in the wild.

Banded Royal ▪ *Rachana jalindra* 20–21mm

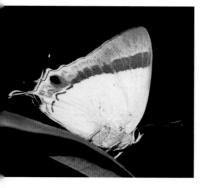

DESCRIPTION Small butterfly. Male upperside metallic blue. Female similar, but has broader black wing borders occupying half of forewing. Underside powdery white, with conspicuous dark brown bands on submarginal regions of both wings. **LARVAL FOODPLANTS** Currently unknown, but probably Loranthaceae and *Macrosolen* (Viscaceae family). **DISTRIBUTION** Subspecies *balabacensis* occurs in Balabac; subspecies *maganda* in Mindanao; subspecies *mindorensis* in Lubang and Mindoro; subspecies *Palawandra* in Dumaran and Palawan; subspecies *shiraishii* in north-west Luzon; subspecies *obsoleta* in Sanga Sanga and Tawi Tawi. **HABITATS** Flies in forested habitats.

Chocolate Royal ▪ *Remelana jangala* 17–20mm

DESCRIPTION Small butterfly. Male dark brown with large, metallic blue patch on forewing, mostly confined to centre part of hindwing. Female purple with broader and wider wings. Male underside reddish-brown; female orange-brown. Cell-end bar on both wings, as well as post-discal narrow band. Tornal region of hindwing has spots and irregular streaks of metallic green scales. **LARVAL FOODPLANTS** *Ixora* species (Rubiaceae family). **DISTRIBUTION** Subspecies *callias* occurs in Mapun; subspecies *esra* in Balabac, Calamian, Dumaran and Palawan. **HABITATS** Flies in primary and secondary forests.

Philippine Chocolate Royal ■ *Remelana westermannii* 18mm

DESCRIPTION Once a subspecies of Chocolate Royal (opposite), but this species is small with brown underside and distinct tornal markings on hindwings. **LARVAL FOODPLANTS** Currently unknown, but probably *Ixora* species (Rubiaceae family). **DISTRIBUTION** Found in Basilan, Bohol, Bongao, Cebu, Camiguin de Luzon, Camotes, Dinagat, Homonhon, Leyte, Lubang, Luzon, Marinduque, Masbate, Mindoro, Mindanao, Negros, Panay, Panaon, Romblon, Samar, Sanga Sanga, Sibuyan, Sibutu and Tawi Tawi. **HABITATS** Mostly seen along forest trails and forest edges.

Common Tit ■ *Hypolycaena erylus* 18mm

DESCRIPTION Small butterfly. Male metallic blue with dark patches positioned centrally on forewing. Female brown with spot on space 2 of hindwing. Underside silvery but darker cell-end bars doubled for both wings. Tornal region of hindwing has spot on space 2 enveloped with orange scales, and spot on space 1a with pale greenish and orange scales. **LARVAL FOODPLANTS** Plants in Combretaceae, Rhizophoraceae and Rubiaceae families. **DISTRIBUTION** Subspecies *tmolus* occurs in Babuyan, Batanes, Catanduanes, Caminguin de Luzon, Luzon, Marinduque, Masbate, Mindoro, Negros, Panay, Romblon and Sibuyan; subspecies *orsiphantus* in Basilan, Camiguin de Mindanao, Dinagat, Leyte, Mindanao and Samar; subspecies *georgius* in Bongao, Jolo, Sanga Sanga, Siasi, Sibutu and Tawi Tawi; subspecies *aimnestus* in Balabac, Cuyo, Dumaran and Palawan. **HABITATS** Flies in various habitats, but mostly encountered along forest trails and forest edges, and nearby in gardens.

Pale Blue Tit ■ *Hypolycaena sipylus* 17mm

DESCRIPTION Small butterfly. Male dark brown with pale bluish patch on median towards margins of hindwings. Underside silvery. Last two spots near costa of forewing not in line with other spots. Space 7 of hindwing has two spots; spot distally larger; spot on space 2 enveloped with orange scales. Female similar, but with rounder wings and less bluish scaling on margins and submargins of hindwings. **LARVAL FOODPLANTS** Buds and

flowers of plants in Rubiaceae (*Ixora* species) and Orchidaceae families. **DISTRIBUTION** Subspecies *tharrytas* occurs in Alabat, Balabac, Basilan, Bohol, Bongao, Cebu, Camiguin de Mindanao, Jolo, Leyte, Lubang, Luzon, Marinduque, Masbate, Mindoro,

Mindanao, Negros, Palawan, Panay, Samar, Sanga Sanga and Sibuyan. **HABITATS** Flies in various habitats, and can be seen perching on shrubs along forest trails and edges. Also flies in home gardens in lowland areas.

Philippine Tit ■ *Hypolycaena ithna* 11–14mm

DESCRIPTION Small butterfly. Looks similar to Pale Blue Tit (above), but has purplish patches on both wings. Female has broader wing margins than male. Underside silvery, and spots on spaces 4 and 5 not in line with rest of spots on forewing. Distal spot on space 7 concave, facing edge of wing, while proximal spot is reduced to dot. **LARVAL FOODPLANTS** Currently unknown, but probably plants in Orchidaceae, Loganiaceae and Rubiaceae families. **DISTRIBUTION** Found in Cebu, Camiguin de Luzon, Dumaran, Leyte, Luzon, Marinduque, Mindoro, Mindanao, Negros, Palawan, Panay, Samar and Sibuyan. **HABITATS** Flies in various habitats, including primary and secondary forests, urban parks and home gardens.

Brown Tit ◾ *Hypolycaena thecloides* 16–18mm

DESCRIPTION Small butterfly. Upperside of male black with whitish scales near anal margins and obvious long tails. Female similar but paler. Underside powdery white with orange colouration on wing borders. Forewing cell-end bar visible, and conspicuous irregular median narrow band on both wings.
LARVAL FOODPLANTS *Flagellaria* (Flagellariaceae family). **DISTRIBUTION** Subspecies *camotana* occurs in Camotes; subspecies *philippina* in Calamian, Cebu, Camiguin de Mindanao, Luzon, Mindoro, Mindanao, Palawan and Sibuyan; subspecies *vardara* in Siargao. **HABITATS** Flies in forested habitats or areas with dense vegetation.

Common Cornelian ◾ *Deudorix epijarbas* 20–22mm

DESCRIPTION Small butterfly. Male bright orange with dark brown forewing margins broadening at apex. Female brown. Underside of male brown-purple-pink. Forewing cell end has white double bar. Spot on space 2 of hindwing surrounded by orange scales.
LARVAL FOODPLANTS Currently unknown, but in other countries caterpillar feeds on various plants, including flowers and fruits in Connaraceae, Sapindaceae and Lythraceae families. **DISTRIBUTION** Found in Bohol, Catanduanes, Cuyo, Cebu, Camiguin de Luzon, Camiguin de Mindanao, Camotes, Leyte, Luzon, Mapun, Marinduque, Masbate, Mindoro, Mindanao, Negros, Palawan, Panay, Samar, Sibutu and Tawi Tawi. **HABITATS** May fly in various habitats, but mostly seen in primary and secondary forests.

Philippine Spark ▪ *Sinthusa natsumiae* 10–13mm

DESCRIPTION Small butterfly. Male dark on forewing, with metallic blue band near base towards tornus, and very inconspicuous purple sheen positioned centrally on wing. Middle

to lower part of hindwing metallic blue. Female similar, but paler and with lesser dark margins on forewings. Post-discal band very close to cell-end bar, in which it attaches on space 4. Spot on space 2 of hindwing large and surrounded with orange scales that connect to spot just protruding at tornus. **LARVAL FOODPLANTS** Currently unknown, but probably plants in Pentaphylacaceae family. **DISTRIBUTION** Subspecies *natsumiae* occurs in Leyte, Luzon, Marinduque, Mindoro, Mindanao, Negros, Panay, Panaon and Samar. **HABITATS** Seen in forested area, so also visits parks and neighbouring gardens to nectar on flowering plants.

Witch

▪ *Araotes lapithis* 13–15mm

DESCRIPTION Small butterfly. Upperside forewing of male brown with inconspicuous dark blue markings near base – very distinct as blue metallic marking on hindwing. Female upperside brown with white patches on anal region of hindwings. Underside orange with white patch marked with irregular-shaped black markings. **LARVAL FOODPLANTS** Currently unknown. **DISTRIBUTION** Subspecies *arianus* occurs in Palawan. **HABITATS** Flies in forested habitats.

Plane ▪ *Bindahara phocides* 18mm

DESCRIPTION Small to medium-sized butterfly. Male upperside black with conspicuous metallic blue rectangular patch on hindwing, and pale orange tail. Female pale brown, with white bands on base of tail. Both sexes have the same patterns on underside, but male is darker, and female is whiter. **LARVAL FOODPLANTS** Currently unknown, but probably *Euonymus* (Celastraceae family). **DISTRIBUTION** Subspecies *phocides* occurs in Sanga Sanga, Sibutu and Tawi Tawi; subspecies *origenes* in Catanduanes, Cebu, Camiguin de Mindanao, Camotes, Luzon, Marinduque, Masbate, Mindoro, Mindanao, Panay, Samar and Sibutu; subspecies *phocas* in Balabac, Calamian, Dumaran and Palawan. **HABITATS** Flies in forested habitats.

Scarlet Flash ▪ *Rapala diecenes* 13–15mm

DESCRIPTION Small butterfly. Male upperside dark brown with conspicuous large orange patch on forewing and hindwing. Female dark brown without orange patches. Underside light brown with orange composition, with narrow median-submarginal bands on both wings. **LARVAL FOODPLANTS** Currently unknown, but probably plants in Anacardiaceae, Malvaceae, Myrtaceae, Euphorbiaceae and Fabaceae families. **DISTRIBUTION** Subspecies *diecenes* occurs in Basilan, Mindanao, Palawan, Sanga Sanga and Sulu. **HABITATS** Rarely seen in the wild, and mostly flies in forested habitats.

Flash ◾ *Rapala caerulescens* 13–18mm

DESCRIPTION Small butterfly. Male dark brown with orange patches on spaces 2 and 1b of forewing and distally on hindwing. Female darker, without orange markings. Characteristics of upperside visible (sometimes not) on underside, but much paler. Spot on space 2 of hindwing has rusty-orange scales on top. **LARVAL FOODPLANTS** Currently unknown, but probably plants in Anacardiaceae, Malvaceae, Myrtaceae, Euphorbiaceae and Fabaceae families. **DISTRIBUTION** Found in Basilan, Cebu, Camiguin de Luzon, Camiguin de Mindanao, Jolo, Leyte, Luzon, Marinduque, Masbate, Mindoro, Mindanao, Negros, Panay, Sibuyan and Siquijor. **HABITATS** Flies in various habitats, such as forest edges and towards lowland urbanized areas.

Tomokoae Flash ◾ *Rapala tomokoae* 13–18mm

DESCRIPTION Small butterfly. Male black with metallic blue colouration occupying half of forewing; hindwing almost completely covered with metallic blue scales. Female similar, but with broader and rounded wings. Underside of both sexes pale brown with greenish composition and conspicuous band on both wings. Tails on hindwings used as defence against predators. **LARVAL FOODPLANTS** Currently unknown, but probably plants in Anacardiaceae, Malvaceae, Myrtaceae, Euphorbiaceae and Fabaceae families. Caterpillar tended by ants. **DISTRIBUTION** Subspecies *tomokoae* occurs in Dinagat, Leyte, Mindanao, Samar and Tawi Tawi; subspecies *bilara* in Bohol; subspecies *takanamii* in Negros, Panay and Siquijor. **HABITATS** Flies in various habitats, including forests and home gardens in urban areas.

Slate Flash

■ *Rapala manea* 13–18mm

DESCRIPTION Small butterfly. Both sexes dark brown, with purplish and greenish composition. Underside dark brown with conspicuous narrow brown band (with white outlines) on both wings. **LARVAL FOODPLANTS** *Lantana camara* (Verbanaceae family). Caterpillars tended by ants. **DISTRIBUTION** Subspecies *ingana* occurs in Dumaran and Palawan; subspecies *philippensis* in Bohol, Dinagat, Leyte, Luzon, Marinduque, Mindoro, Mindanao, Negros, Panay, Sibuyan, Sibutu and Tawi Tawi. **HABITATS** Flies in various habitats, such as forest edges and towards home gardens in lowland areas.

Metalmarks

Larger Harlequin

■ *Taxila haquinus* 22–23mm

DESCRIPTION Medium-sized butterfly in which base colouration of upperside of male is dark brown, with pale brownish-orange colouration on apices. Female has orange with white band on subapical region, and black spots distributed throughout wings. Underside of male dark orange with black and metallic white spots. Similar characteristics in female on upperside, but spots more pronounced on underside. **LARVAL FOODPLANTS** *Ardisia* species (Myrsinaceae family). **DISTRIBUTION** Subspecies *palawanicus* occurs in Balabac and Palawan. **HABITATS** Flies in forested areas of Palawan.

Spotted Judy ■ *Abisara geza* 23mm

DESCRIPTION Medium-sized butterfly. Male and female have almost the same colouration, which is reddish-brown with white patch on subapical regions of forewings. Female paler. Hindwings have five visible spots on submarginal regions. Similar characteristics on underside. **LARVAL FOODPLANTS** *Embelia* species (Myrsinaceae family). **DISTRIBUTION** Subspecies *aja* occurs in Balabac, Calamian, Dumaran and Palawan. **HABITATS** Flies in forested habitats, and may also visit nearby home gardens.

SKIPPERS

Pale Awlet ■ *Bibasis gomata* 25–28mm

DESCRIPTION Small butterfly with stout body. Male has conspicuous dirty-white and brownish streaks on uppersides of wings. Similar characteristics on underside, but forewings have more white scales on basal extending to median regions. Anal margins of hindwings have yellow and pale bluish scales. Upperside of female darker, with metallic greenish scales on basal to post-basal regions of wings, and then dark blue to purplish distally. Forewings have two conspicuous oblong white spots on spaces 2 and 3. Underside similar, but striations more pronounced and more metallic greenish scales, especially on costa, apex and marginal regions of forewings. **LARVAL FOODPLANTS** *Schefflera*, *Trevesia*, *Heptapluron*, *Horsfieldia* and *Embelia* species. **DISTRIBUTION** Subspecies *lorquini* occurs in Calamian, Cebu, Camiguin de Luzon, Leyte, Luzon, Marinduque, Mindoro, Mindanao, Negros, Palawan, Panay and Pollilo. **HABITATS** Flies mostly in forested habitats, and visits flowering plants in nearby home gardens. Flies briefly, then perches underneath leaf.

Orange Awlet ▪ *Bibasis harisa* 25mm

DESCRIPTION Small butterfly. Upperside of male reddish-brown, while female is metallic purplish with bluish and greenish composition. Underside of both sexes dark brown with reddish composition, and narrow, yellow-orange streaks. **LARVAL FOODPLANTS** *Zingiber*, *Arhtrophyllum* and *Urophyllum* species. **DISTRIBUTION** Subspecies *consobrina* occurs in Sanga Sanga and Sibutu; subspecies *pala* in Dumaran and Palawan; subspecies *grandis* in Dinagat, Leyte and Samar. **HABITATS** Flies in forested areas of Palawan.

Orange-tailed Awl ▪ *Bibasis sena* 20mm

DESCRIPTION Small butterfly with stout body. Base colour brown, but with oranges scales on anal to tornal regions of hindwings. Very pale white band sometimes observable on both wings. On underside, paler brown colouration with very conspicuous white band that looks like a 'mermaid', of which head part terminates into pinkish-purplish scales on forewings, while tail part terminates into yellow scales on hindwings. Orange scales on anal and tornal regions of hindwings visible. **LARVAL FOODPLANTS** *Pisonia* (Nyctaginaceae), *Combretum* (Combretaceae) and *Hiptage* (Malpighiaceae). **DISTRIBUTION** Subspecies *palawana* occurs in Bohol, Bongao, Boracay, Calamian, Cebu, Homonhon, Leyte, Luzon, Marinduque, Masbate, Mindoro, Mindanao, Negros, Palawan, Panay, Polillo, Samar, Sanga Sanga, Sibuyan, Sibutu and Tawi Tawi. **HABITATS** Probably flies in various habitats, but mostly encountered in forested areas.

Common Banded Awl ▪ *Hasora chromus* 22mm

DESCRIPTION Small, dark brown butterfly with purple to bluish composition on undersides of wings. Apical small spot can be absent, and females have yellowish irregular spots on spaces 2 and 3 of forewing. Underside hindwing has conspicuous straight white band (with purple and bluish composition) on median region. **LARVAL FOODPLANTS** *Pongamia* (Fabaceae family). **DISTRIBUTION** Subspecies *chromus* occurs in Basilan, Bongao, Leyte, Luzon, Marinduque, Mindanao, Negros, Samar, Sanga Sanga, Sibuyan, Tawi Tawi and Ticao. **HABITATS** Flies in various habitats, including forests and down to coastal areas, especially near *Pongamia* trees.

White-banded Awl ▪ *Hasora taminatus* 20–21mm

DESCRIPTION Small butterfly. Underside forewing brown, but with very pronounced metallic bluish-purplish to greenish scales on costal region extending to middle (the cell) of wing. Hindwings have similar scaling on basal, terminating on white band, although dusting can be seen on marginal and submarginal regions. Tornal region has broad black patch with white scaling near anal margin. Narrow white band starting from black patch terminating on space 7, and with visible white dusting on space 8. **LARVAL**

FOODPLANTS *Millettia*, *Dalbergia* and *Pongamia* (all Fabaceae family). **DISTRIBUTION** Subspecies *malayana* occurs in Balabac, South Palawan, Sibutu, and Tawi Tawi; subspecies *padma* in Basilan, Bohol, Bongao, Cebu, Camiguin de Luzon, Dinagat, Homonhon, Leyte, Luzon, Marinduque, Masbate, Mindoro, Mindanao, Negros, North Palawan, Panay, Panaon, Romblon, Sibuyan and Ticao. **HABITATS** Flies in various habitats, such as primary and secondary forests, and also in cultivated places and towards coastal areas.

Yellow-banded Awl ■ *Hasora schoenherr* 20–22mm

DESCRIPTION Small butterfly. Upperside of forewing brown but with conspicuous yellow scaling on space 1. Three white patches with different shapes on median region: parallelogram shape on space 2; rectangular shape on space 3; white patch on cell. Also three conspicuous white rectangular patches on subapical region, and very tiny white spot on space 5, which is almost attached to one of the three rectangular spots. Hindwing has yellow scales and hairs surrounded with brownish band from costa arching on apex to marginal region, and terminating on tornal region.

Underside similar to upperside, but with paler and less pronounced characteristics, and almost dusted with yellow. Tornal region has black patch. **LARVAL FOODPLANTS** *Fordia* and *Spatholobus* (both Fabaceae family). **DISTRIBUTION** Subspecies *saida* occurs in Bohol, Camiguin de Mindanao, Camiguin de Luzon, Cuyo, Leyte, Luzon, Marinduque, Masbate, Mindoro, Mindanao, Negros, Panay, Panaon, Samar and Sibuyan; subspecies *chuza* in Balabac, Palawan and Dumaran; subspecies *babuyana* in Babuyan islands. **HABITATS** Flies in various habitats, such as forests, and towards cultivated places and coastal areas.

Lesser Awl ■ *Hasora mixta* 22–24mm

DESCRIPTION Small butterfly. Upperside of male dark brown. Underside has similar characteristic, but with purplish tinge and black patch on tornal region of hindwing. In female, upperside dark brown, but with brown hairs and scales proximally or near body. Four visible white patches: very tiny spot on space 6; squarish shape on space 2;

narrow, rectangular shape on space 3; patch on cell. Similar characteristics on underside, but with more pronounced 'mixing' of different dusted colours such as purple, pink, brown and blue. Space 1 of forewings has white scaling. **LARVAL FOODPLANTS** *Derris*, *Millettia* and *Pongamia* (all Fabaceae family). **DISTRIBUTION** Subspecies *mixta* occurs in Babuyan, Basilan, Biliran, Bongao, Cebu, Camiguin de Mindanao, Dinagat, Homonhon, Leyte, Luzon, Marinduque, Masbate, Mindoro, Mindanao, Negros, Panay, Panaon, Samar, Sibuyan and Siasi; subspecies *prabha* in Balabac, Busuanga, Dumaran, Palawan and Sanga Sanga. **HABITATS** Flies in various habitats, such as forests, and towards cultivated places and coastal areas.

Common Awl ■ *Hasora badra* 24mm

DESCRIPTION Small butterfly. Upperside of male looks similar to Lesser Awl's (p. 137); most of the differences found on underside. Underside hindwing has white cell spot and white 'hook-shaped' band on space 1b. Female similar to Lesser, but subapical region has three tiny spots (sometimes only one on space 6) on spaces 6, 7 and 8. Hindwing has white cell spot and white 'hook shape' (sometimes just looks like a patch) on space 1b. **LARVAL FOODPLANTS** *Derris*, *Millettia* and *Pongamia* (all Fabaceae family). **DISTRIBUTION** Subspecies *badra* occurs in Balabac, Calamian, Dumaran and Palawan. **HABITATS** Flies in various habitats, such as forests and towards cultivated places and in coastal areas.

Plain Banded Awl ■ *Hasora vitta* 24–25mm

DESCRIPTION Small butterfly. Upperside of male dark brown with two conspicuous irregular yellow spots on median of forewing and tiny yellow dot on subapex. These characteristics sometimes reduced or not well pronounced. Underside similar to other species of *Hasora*, and two tiny spots still visible, but there is a 'zigzag' narrow white band on cell spaces 1a and 1b. Basal to post-basal region of hindwing dusted with brown and metallic green. Conspicuous white band visible starting from cell space 8 and extending down to black patch on tornal region, then continuing to anal margin. Female's upperside looks similar to male's, but cell space 3 has rectangular white patch instead of spot, and

there is an additional similar shape to the latter on cell space 2. Underside similar to upperside, but forewings have mixed dusting instead of plain brown. As in male, white band starting on cell space 8 extending to tornal black patch, then terminating on anal margin. **LARVAL FOODPLANTS** *Derris*, *Endosamara*, *Milletia*, *Phaseolodes*, *Pongamia* and *Spatholobus* (all Fabaceae family). **DISTRIBUTION** Subspecies *proximata* occurs in Balabac, Camiguin de Luzon, Dumaran, Luzon, Mindoro, Mindanao and Palawan. **HABITATS** Flies in various habitats, such as forests and towards cultivated places and in coastal areas.

Pied Flat ▪ *Coladenia similis* 17mm

DESCRIPTION Small, dark brown butterfly with three small white spots on subapical region of forewing; spot near costa larger than other two spots below it. Four conspicuous yellowish markings on median section, of which irregular square-shaped spot on cell is largest. Underside similar to upperside, but paler and with visible faded black spots. **LARVAL FOODPLANTS** *Connarus semidecandrus* (Connaraceae family). **DISTRIBUTION** Found in Camiguin de Mindanao, Luzon, Marinduque and Mindanao. **HABITATS** Flies in forested areas, and can be seen flying swiftly but over short distances along forest trails.

Corona Flat ▪ *Gerosis corona* 17–18mm

DESCRIPTION Small black butterfly with conspicuous large, circular yellow (white on underside) patch on hindwing in male; white patch in female. Median of forewing has two large spots, and another one just near submarginal region. Subapical region has three white spots (middle spot smaller). **LARVAL FOODPLANTS** *Albrus* and *Dalbergia* (both Fabaceae family). **DISTRIBUTION** Subspecies *corona* occurs in Alabat, Camiguin de Mindanao, Leyte, Luzon, Masbate, Marinduque, Mindoro (excluding Mt Halcon area), Mindanao, Panay and Samar. **HABITATS** Flies in forested areas.

Common Snow Flat ■ *Tagiades japetus* 17–23mm

DESCRIPTION Small, dark brown butterfly with four (sometimes five on underside) tiny spots on subapex of forewing, and three larger spots on median region. Spot on cell dented on both sides. Underside the same, but with whitish scaling on most of hindwing. **LARVAL FOODPLANTS** Various plants, especially in Dioscoreaceae, Convolvulaceae, Dipterocarpaceae, Roxburghiaceae and Smilacaceae families. **DISTRIBUTION** Subspecies *titus* occurs in Babuyan, Basilan, Biliran, Bohol, Bongao, Calamian, Cebu, Camiguin

de Luzon, Camiguin de Mindanao, Camotes, Dinagat, Guimaras, Leyte, Lubang, Luzon, Masbate, Mindoro, Mindanao, Negros, Palawan, Panay, Polillo, Samar, Sanga Sanga, Siargao, Sibuyan, Sibutu, Siquijor and Tawi Tawi. **HABITATS** Flies in various habitats, and can be seen nectaring on flowering plants in open spaces and gardens. Flies swiftly for short periods, then perches under leaf.

Large Snow Flat ■ *Tagiades gana* 21mm

DESCRIPTION Small, dark brown butterfly similar to Common Snow Flat (above), but with narrower subapical spots and median spots absent. Anal margin on hindwing has white scaling with black spots. Underside the same, but paler and with white scaling occupying most of hindwing and black spots on margin. **LARVAL FOODPLANTS** *Dioscorea* (Dioscoreaceae family). **DISTRIBUTION** Subspecies *gana* occurs in Palawan, Sanga Sanga, Sibutu and Tawi Tawi; subspecies *elegans* in Basilan, Biliran, Bohol, Balut, Cebu, Camiguin de Mindanao, Camotes, Dinagat, Leyte, Luzon, Marinduque, Masbate, Mindanao, Negros, Panay, Panaon, Polillo, Samar, Siargao and Sibuyan. **HABITATS** Flies in forested areas and open spaces similarly to Common.

Trebellius Snow Flat ■ *Tagiades trebellius* 18–20mm

DESCRIPTION Small butterfly that is darker than other *Tagiades* species. Forewing upperside has five conspicuous spots on subapex, and 2–3 spots on median region. Hindwing has large, irregular-shaped white patch with black spots near wing margin. Underside similar, but hindwing has white scaling on most of wing, and black spots on margin and towards median region. **LARVAL FOODPLANTS** *Dioscorea piscatorum* (Dioscoreaceae family). **DISTRIBUTION** Subspecies *martinus* occurs in Babuyan, Basilan, Batan, Bohol, Cebu, Camiguin de Mindanao, Dinagat, Homonhon, Leyte, Luzon, Marinduque, Mindanao, Mindoro, Negros, Palawan, Panay, Polillo, Samar, Sanga Sanga, Sibuyan, Tawi Tawi and Ticao. **HABITATS** Flies in forested habitats, and can also be seen nectaring on plants in barren and open spaces near forests.

Banded Angle
■ *Odontoptilum pygela* 17mm

DESCRIPTION Small, rusty-brown butterfly with heavy white scales on hindwing. Distinguishable by pointy edges of hindwing. Bell-shaped curve marking on median region of hindwing. **LARVAL FOODPLANTS** Various plants in Bombaceae, Malvaceae, Sapindaceae, Sterculiaceae and Tiliaceae families. **DISTRIBUTION** Subspecies *pygela* occurs in Palawan; subspecies *tawita* in Sanga Sanga and Tawi Tawi. **HABITATS** Flies in various habitats, including forests and home gardens.

Blue Scrub Hopper
■ *Aeromachus plumbeola* 11–12mm

DESCRIPTION Small, dark brown butterfly. Uppersides of wings have pale bluish scales. Can be mistaken for Lesser Grass Blue (p. 105) due to size and colour. Scrub Hopper (below) does not have pale bluish scales. **LARVAL FOODPLANTS** Plants in grass family (Poaceae). **DISTRIBUTION** Found in Basilan, Biliran, Dinagat, Leyte, Luzon, Masbate, Mindoro, Mindanao, Negros, Panay and Samar. **HABITATS** Flies in various habitats, including roadsides, open spaces and home gardens.

Scrub Hopper ■ *Aeromachus musca* 10–11mm

DESCRIPTION Small, dark brown butterfly similar to Blue Scrub Hopper (above), but lacks pale bluish scaling on wings. **LARVAL FOODPLANTS** Plants in grass family (Poaceae). **DISTRIBUTION** Found in Cebu, Leyte, Luzon, Mindoro, Mindanao, Negros, Samar and Siargao. **HABITATS** Flies in various habitats, including forests and lowland gardens.

Common Ace ■ *Halpe luteisquama* 14–16mm

DESCRIPTION Small, rusty-brown butterfly with 2–3 subapical white spots (topmost spot sometimes tiny or absent). Two bullet-shaped white spots on median of forewing. Underside similar to upperside, but hindwing has syringe-like markings from anal region towards apex. **LARVAL FOODPLANTS** Certain grass species (Poaceae). **DISTRIBUTION** Found in Basilan, Cebu, Camiguin de Luzon, Dinagat, Jolo, Leyte, Luzon, Marinduque, Mindoro, Mindanao, Negros, Palawan, Panay, Samar, Sibuyan, Sibutu and Tawi Tawi. **HABITATS** Flies in various habitats, including forests and home gardens.

Palawan Ace

■ *Halpe toxopea* 12–14mm

DESCRIPTION Small, dark brown butterfly with rusty composition. Similar to Common Ace (above), but smaller in size, and hindwing underside median markings of various sizes not aligned together. **LARVAL FOODPLANTS** Certain grass species (Poaceae family). **DISTRIBUTION** Found in Calamian, Dumaran and Palawan. **HABITATS** Flies in various habitats, including forests and home gardens.

Narrow-banded Velvet Bob ▪ *Koruthaialos rubecula* 15–19mm

DESCRIPTION Small butterfly. Dark brown to black, and distinguishable by orange band or patch on forewing, which can be absent in some individuals. **LARVAL FOODPLANTS**

Plants in Musaceae family. **DISTRIBUTION** Subspecies *atra* occurs in Basilan, Bongao, Cebu, Leyte, Masbate, Mindanao, Negros and Samar; subspecies *luzonensis* in Catanduanes, Luzon, Marinduque and Polillo; subspecies *ponta* in Balabac, Calamian and Palawan. **HABITATS** Flies in forested areas. Can be seen perching on leaves, opening and closing wings occasionally.

Chocolate Demon ▪ *Ancistroides nigrita* 23–26mm

DESCRIPTION Small to medium-sized butterfly that looks similar to *Psolos* and *Koruthaialos* species, but relatively larger and forewing more triangular. **LARVAL FOODPLANTS** Plants in Zingiberaceae family. **DISTRIBUTION** Subspecies *fumatus* occurs in Babuyan, Balabac, Basilan, Biliran, Bohol, Cebu, Camiguin de Mindanao, Guimaras, Leyte, Luzon, Masbate, Mindoro, Mindanao, Negros, Palawan, Panay, Samar, Sarangani and Sibuyan. **HABITATS** Flies swiftly in forested habitats, and can be seen perching on leaves or feeding on dung.

Common Banded Demon ■ *Notocrypta paralysos* 15–19mm

DESCRIPTION Small, dark brown butterfly. This species does not have apical spots on cell spaces 6,7 and 8. Forewing underside white band does not generally extend above radius to costa, although in some cases it does, but not very pronounced, with slightly white dusting.

LARVAL FOODPLANTS *Zingiber* and *Curcuma* (both Zingiberaceae family), and species in other families, including Costaceae, Marantaceae and Musaceae.
DISTRIBUTION Subspecies *varians* occurs in Sibutu; subspecies *volux* in Basilan, Biliran, Cebu, Camiguin de Luzon, Caminguin de Mindanao, Dinagat, Homonhon, Leyte, Luzon, Marinduque, Masbate, Mindoro, Mindanao, Negros, Panay, Polillo, Samar, Sanga Sanga, Sibuyan and Tawi Tawi; subspecies *chunda* in Balabac, Calamian and Palawan. **HABITATS** Flies in forested habitats, and can be seen flying on forest trails and in clearings, then perching on shrubs. Can also be seen in home gardens near forests.

Spotted Demon ■ *Notocrypta feisthamelii* 20–21mm

DESCRIPTION Small butterfly that looks similar to Common Banded Demon (above), but underside white band extends towards costa of forewing. White spots on post-median region of forewing and purplish-white scaling on underside marginal and submarginal regions of both wings. **LARVAL FOODPLANTS** *Zingiber*, *Elettaria* and *Curcuma* (all in Zingiberaceae family). **DISTRIBUTION** Subspecies *alinkara* occurs in Babuyan, Batanes, Biliran, Bohol, Calamian, Catanduanes, Cebu, Dinagat, Leyte, Luzon, Marinduque, Mindoro, Mindanao, Negros, Palawan, Panay, Panaon, Polillo, Samar and Sibuyan. **HABITATS** Flies in forested habitats and nearby home gardens. Exhibits similar behaviour to Common.

Dark Grass Bob ■ *Suada catoleucos* 16mm

DESCRIPTION Small butterfly. Wing base colour brown with very conspicuous white patch covering hindwing. Forewing has tiny dots on cell spaces 6 and 7, and very tiny white spot on cell space 8. Female may also have white dots on cell spaces 2 and 3. Underside brown with white patch near margin of forewing; most of hindwing dusted with white. Male looks like paler version of female. **LARVAL FOODPLANTS** Feeds on plants in grass family (Poaceae). **DISTRIBUTION** Found in Mindanao and Palawan. **HABITATS** Flies in various habitats, such as forests and agricultural areas (lowland).

Grass Bob ■ *Suada albinus* 16–17mm

DESCRIPTION Small, dark brown butterfly with three conspicuous white spots on median region of forewing. Hindwing has white patch that occupies half of wing. **LARVAL FOODPLANTS** Feeds on plants in grass family (Poaceae). **DISTRIBUTION** Found in Basilan, Leyte, Luzon, Mindanao and Polillo. **HABITATS** Flies in various habitats, such as forests and agricultural areas (lowland).

Small Palm Bob ■ *Suastus minutus* 13–14mm

DESCRIPTION Small butterfly with mostly brown base colour. Forewing upperside has conspicuous spots of varying shapes, especially on spaces 2 and 3, including spot on lower part of cell. These three spots very close to each other. Other tiny spots on upper part of cell and on space 6. Spots visible from underside, and there is a white patch on mid-cell space 1b (well pronounced in Oriental Palm Bob *Suastus gremius*). Hindwing brown dusted with white, and brownish spots can be more or less pronounced. **LARVAL FOODPLANTS** Palms (Arecaceae family). **DISTRIBUTION** Subspecies *scopas* occurs in Dumaran and Palawan; subspecies *compactus* in Calamian. **HABITATS** Flies in forested areas and nearby clearings or open spaces.

Small Palm Flitter ■ *Zographetus rama* 15mm

DESCRIPTION Small butterfly with similar characteristics to other species. The sole difference is that spots on forewings are pale yellow and mostly less pronounced than in other species. **LARVAL FOODPLANTS** Various plants, including species in Fabaceae, Gnetaceae and Sterculiaceae families. **DISTRIBUTION** Found in Balabac, Mindoro, Mindanao, Negros, Palawan and Samar. **HABITATS** Flies in forested areas. Can also be seen feeding on dung.

Tree Flitter

■ *Hyarotis adrastus* 18mm

DESCRIPTION Small brown butterfly (female pale brown) with conspicuous spots on spaces 3 and 6–8. Spots on cell and space 2 almost fused. Undersides of hindwings have pointy white band. **LARVAL FOODPLANTS** Palms (Arecaceae family). **DISTRIBUTION** Subspecies *praba* occurs in Calamian, Mindanao and Palawan. **HABITATS** Flies in forested areas, including clearings and open spaces with flowering plants.

Giant Redeye ■ *Gangara thyrsis* 33–38mm

DESCRIPTION Small butterfly with well-pronounced spots on spaces 2, 3, 6, 7 and 8, as well as large cell spot. Underside has pale purplish banding on hindwing. Spots on spaces 6–8 surrounded by purplish scales. **LARVAL FOODPLANTS** Plants in Arecaceae and Musaceae families. **DISTRIBUTION** Subspecies *thyrsis* occurs in Palawan; subspecies *philippensis* in Bohol, Camiguin de Luzon, Leyte, Luzon, Mindoro, Mindanao, Panaon, Samar and Sibuyan; subspecies *magnificens* in Negros and Panay. **HABITATS** Flies in various habitats, such as home gardens and cleared areas.

Banded Redeye ■ *Gangara lebadea* 25–30mm

DESCRIPTION Small butterfly. Male spotless but with very conspicuous pink band on undersides of hindwings and forewings. Female similar to Giant Redeye (opposite), but without spots on spaces 6–8.
LARVAL FOODPLANTS Plants in Arecaceae and Musaceae families.
DISTRIBUTION Subspecies *janlourensi* occurs in Leyte; subspecies *guyi* in Dumaran and Palawan. **HABITATS** Flies in various habitats, such as home gardens and cleared areas.

Banana Skipper ■ *Erionota thrax* 28–38mm

DESCRIPTION Medium-sized brown butterfly with large spots on cell, and spaces 2 and 3 (smaller). No spots on spaces 6–8. Apex of forewing acute or pointy, and termen straight.
LARVAL FOODPLANTS Plants in Arecaceae, Musaceae and Zingiberaceae families.
DISTRIBUTION Subspecies *thrax* occurs in Cebu, Camotes, Luzon (excluding north and north-west Luzon), Marinduque, Masbate, Mindoro, Negros, Palawan, Panay, Polillo, Sibuyan, Sibutu and Tawi Tawi; subspecies *mindana* in Dinagat, Homonhon, Jolo, Leyte, Mindanao and Samar; subspecies *alexandra* in north and north-west Luzon. **HABITATS** Rather common butterfly that flies in various habitats, including home gardens, agricultural land, and open or cleared areas.

Hoary Palmer ■ *Unkana ambasa* 23–27mm

DESCRIPTION Small, dark brown butterfly with white markings on forewings. Forewing cell has dented, square-shaped (sometimes irregular) marking and another two beside it. Subapical region has at least five white spots, of which the first three near costa are closer to each other. Female has white patch on uppersides of hindwings, which is almost absent in male. **LARVAL FOODPLANTS** Plants in Pandanaceae family. **DISTRIBUTION** Subspecies *batara* occurs in Sanga Sanga, Sibutu and Tawi Tawi; subspecies *palawana* in Palawan; subspecies *mindanaensis* in Bohol, Camiguin de Luzon, Dinagat, Homonhon, Leyte, Luzon, Mindoro, Mindanao, Negros, Panay, Samar and Sibuyan. **HABITATS** Flies in various habitats at higher to lower elevations.

Banded Palmer
■ *Acerbas duris* 19–22mm

DESCRIPTION Dark brown to black, and distinguishable by broad white band on hindwing. Forewing has three tiny spots on subapex, and three larger spots on median, of which one spot is in cell. **LARVAL FOODPLANTS** Probably plants in Arecaceae family. **DISTRIBUTION** Subspecies *duris* occurs in Cebu, Camiguin de Luzon, Camiguin de Mindanao, Leyte, Luzon, Marinduque, Masbate, Mindoro, Mindanao, Negros and Panaon. **HABITATS** Flies in forested areas, and can be seen flying fast along forest trails.

Green-striped Palmer
■ *Pirdana hyela* 20–24mm

DESCRIPTION Small butterfly in which upperside of both sexes is brown with gentle sheen of bluish colouration (more pronounced in female than male). Underside of hindwing greenish-bluish. Tornal region has orange fringes. **LARVAL FOODPLANTS** *Dracaena*, *Cordyline* and *Peliosanthes* (all in Asparagaceae family). **DISTRIBUTION** Subspecies *hyela* occurs in Leyte, Luzon, Mindanao and Palawan. **HABITATS** Flies in forested habitats.

Luzon Grass Dart ■ *Taractrocera luzonensis* 9–12mm

DESCRIPTION Small, dark brown butterfly with orange markings on wings. On forewing, cell has orange bands that end with heart-shaped marking near subapical region. Orange markings of various sizes form band on post-median region. Hindwing has orange band on median region, and some orange spots near bases of wings. Underside similar to upperside, but with more orange scaling. **LARVAL FOODPLANTS** Grasses (Poaceae family). **DISTRIBUTION** Subspecies *luzonensis* occurs in Balabac, Basilan, Cebu, Dinagat, Leyte, Luzon, Mapun, Marinduque, Masbate, Mindoro, Mindanao, Negros, Palawan, Panay, Samar and Sibuyan. **HABITATS** Mostly flies in grassy environments such as ball fields, roadsides, home gardens and forest edges.

Common Dartlet ■ *Oriens gola* 11–13mm

DESCRIPTION Small, dark brown butterfly similar to Luzon Grass Dart (p. 151), but with orange band positioned inwardly on median and fusing with heart-shaped marking

on cell end. Median orange band looks as though it has pointy dents, one pointing to margin of forewing, and the other to hindwing. Underside similar, but with more orange scaling on upper half of both wings and black scaling on lower half. **LARVAL FOODPLANTS** Grasses (Poaceae family). **DISTRIBUTION** Subspecies *pseudolus* occurs in Balabac, Calamian, Luzon and Palawan. **HABITATS** Flies in various habitats, including forests and towards lowland areas. Rarely seen and sometimes flies with Luzon Grass Dart.

Dark Palm Dart ■ *Telicota ancilla* 13–18mm

DESCRIPTION Small, dark brown butterfly with orange markings on both wings. On forewing, five rectangular-shaped orange markings on post-median region form band, which is joined by another orange marking on costa towards subapex. Cell has orange scaling, and there is a conspicuous shiny blank band on median (looks like slanted 'L'-

shaped marking). Hindwing has orange band and orange spots on cell. Female similar to male but paler. **LARVAL FOODPLANTS** Plants in Arecaceae, Flagellariaceae and Poaceae families. **DISTRIBUTION** Subspecies *minda* occurs in Babuyan, Basilan, Cebu, Homonhon, Leyte, Luzon, Marinduque, Masbate, Mindoro, Mindanao, Negros, Palawan, Panay, Romblon, Samar, Sibuyan and Ticao. **HABITATS** Flies in forested habitats, and can be seen nectaring on flowering plants on trails of forest edges. Also found in lowland areas.

Plain Palm Dart ■ *Cephrenes acalle* 16–24mm

DESCRIPTION Small, black and orange butterfly. Male similar to Dark Palm Dart (opposite), but relatively larger and orange band on post-median region wider (especially bottom markings) and weakly joined with orange band on costa. Black median band shorter and less pronounced. Orange bands on hindwing almost joined due to paler black lines, and cell orange marking more faded and larger. Underside orange with smeared black scaling on margins and submargins of forewings, and bases of both wings have black scaling forming faded band. Female darker, with some orange markings much reduced. **LARVAL FOODPLANTS** Palms (Arecaceae family). **DISTRIBUTION** Subspecies *chrysozona* occurs in Bohol, Cebu, Camiguin de Mindanao, Camotes, Dinagat, Leyte, Luzon, Marinduque, Mindoro, Mindanao, Negros, Panay, Polillo, Samar and Sibuyan; subspecies *kliana* in Balabac, Bongao, Mapun, Palawan, Sanga Sanga, Sitangkai and Sibutu. **HABITATS** Flies in various habitats, such as forests and towards home gardens in lowland areas.

Rice Swift ■ *Borbo cinnara* 16mm

DESCRIPTION Small, dark brown butterfly with distinct white spots on wings. On forewing, three tiny white spots near subapical region, followed by another three spots below, with bottom-most white spot the largest. Yellow spot below large white spot. Faded white spots on hindwing, but more visible from underside. Underside pale brown with conspicuous black scaling near base of forewing, and three white spots on post-median region. **LARVAL FOODPLANTS** Grasses (Poaceae family). **DISTRIBUTION** Found in Balabac, Batanes, Camiguin de Mindanao, Jolo, Leyte, Lubang, Luzon, Masbate, Mindoro, Mindanao, Negros, Palawan, Panay, Samar, Sanga Sanga, Sibutu and Tawi Tawi. **HABITATS** Flies in various habitats, such as forests and home gardens in lowland areas.

Small Branded Swift ■ *Pelopidas mathias* 16–19mm

DESCRIPTION Small brown butterfly with greenish composition. Conspicuous spots on median region of forewing, and two spots on cell. Hindwing underside has inconspicuous

small median white spots, and largest spot on forewing is rectangular. **LARVAL FOODPLANTS** Certain grass species (Poaceae family). **DISTRIBUTION** Subspecies *mathias* occurs in Bohol, Cebu, Camiguin de Luzon, Camiguin de Mindanao, Camotes, Guimaras, Homonhon, Jolo, Leyte, Luzon, Marinduque, Masbate, Mindoro, Negros, Palawan, Panay, Panaon, Samar, Siargao and Tawi Tawi. **HABITATS** Flies in various habitats, such as forest trails and forest edges, down to lowland home gardens.

EX – Extinct
EW – Extinct in the wild
EN – Endangered
VU – Vulnerable
NT – Near Threatened
LC – Least Concern

DD – Data Deficient
NE – Not Evaluated
LR-cd – Lower Risk/Conservation Dependent
I – Intermediate
R – Rare
N/A – Not available

The status of each butterfly presented here is from CITES, IUCN, and Danielsen & Treadaway 2004, and may refer to the species or subspecies. The common names are some of the suggested names for most Philippine endemic species. However, they are subject to change.

Common Names	Scientific Names	Status	Endemicity
PAPILIONIDAE (Birdwings & Swallowtails)			
Chail Swordtail	Arisbe aristeus	N/A	
Spotted Jay	Arisbe arycles	N/A	
Veined Jay	Arisbe bathycles	N/A	
The Green Swordtail	Arisbe decolor	N/A	
The Malayan Zebra	Arisbe delesserti	N/A	
Common Jay	Arisbe doson	N/A	
Euphrates Swordtail	Arisbe euphrates	N/A	Endemic
The Mindanao Swordtail	Arisbe euphratoides	CR	Endemic
Great Jay	Arisbe eurypylus	N/A	
The Blue Jay	Arisbe evemon	N/A	
The Philippine Jay	Arisbe idaeoides	VU	Endemic
Lesser Zebra	Arisbe macareus	N/A	
The Palawan Jay	Arisbe megaera	VU	Endemic
The Philippine Zebra	Arisbe stratocles	N/A	Endemic
Tailed Jay	Graphium agamemnon	N/A	
Eastern Olive Triangle	Graphium codrus	N/A	
Empedovana Triangle	Graphium empedovana	N/A	
Apo Swallowtail	Graphium sandawanum	LR-cd	Endemic
Common Bluebottle	Graphium sarpedon	N/A	
White Dragontail	Lamproptera curius	N/A	
Green Dragontail	Lamproptera meges	N/A	
Luzon Peacock Swallowtail	Achillides chikae	Appendix I, CITES; LR-cd; VU	Endemic
Jungle Jade	Achillides karna	N/A	
Banded Peacock	Achillides palinurus	N/A	
Paris Peacock	Achillides paris	N/A	
The Mindanaoo Mime	Chilasa carolinensis	CR	Endemic
Common Mime	Chilasa clytia	N/A	
Osman's Mime	Chilasa osmana	CR	Endemic
Great Blue Mime	Chilasa paradoxa	VU	
Scarlet Mormon	Menelaides deiphobus	N/A	
Red Helen	Menelaides helenus	N/A	
Banded Mormon	Menelaides hipponous	N/A	
Luzviae Mormon	Menelaides luzviae	CR	Endemic
Great Yellow Mormon	Menelaides memnon	N/A	
Common Mormon	Menelaides polytes	N/A	
Antonio Mormon	Papilio antonio	EN	Endemic
Common Lime Swallowtail	Papilio demoleus	N/A	
Banded Swallowtail	Papilio demolion	N/A	
Asian Swallowtail	Papilio xuthus	NT	
Batwing	Atrophaneura semperi	N/A	Endemic
Yellow-Bodied Club-Tail	Balignina neptunus	VU; EN	
Black Rose	Pachliopta antiphus	VU; EN	

Common Names	Scientific Names	Status	Endemicity
Common Rose	*Pachliopta aristolochiae*	N/A	
Pink Rose	*Pachliopta atropos*	VU	Endemic
Philippine Pink Rose	*Pachliopta kotzebuea*	N/A	Endemic
Leyte Pink Rose	*Pachliopta leytensis*	N/A	Endemic
The Eastern Pink Rose	*Pachliopta mariae*	N/A	Endemic
The Mindanao Pink Rose	*Pachliopta phlegon*	VU	Endemic
Schadenbergi's Pink Rose	*Pachliopta schadenbergi*	VU	Endemic
Strand's Pink Rose	*Pachliopta strandi*	EN	Endemic
Rajah Brooke's Birdwing	*Trogonoptera brookiana*	Appendix II, CITES	
Palawan Birdwing	*Trogonoptera trojana*	Appendix II, CITES	Endemic
Magellan Birdwing	*Troides magellanus*	Appendix II, CITES	
Golden Birdwing	*Troides rhadamantus*	Appendix II, CITES	
PIERIDAE (Whites, Yellows, Orange Tips & Sulphurs)			
Lemon Emigrant	*Catopsilia pomona*	N/A	
Mottled Emigrant	*Catopsilia pyranthe*	N/A	
Orange Emigrant	*Catopsilia scylla*	N/A	
Scalloped Grass Yellow	*Eurema alitha*	N/A	
Anderson's Grass Yellow	*Eurema andersonii*	N/A	
Three-Spot Grass Yellow	*Eurema blanda*	N/A	
Small Grass Yellow	*Eurema brigitta*	N/A	
Common Grass Yellow	*Eurema hecabe*	N/A	
Hiurai's Grass Yellow	*Eurema hiurai*	N/A	Endemic
The Scarce Grass Yellow	*Eurema lacteola*	N/A	
Spotless Grass Yellow	*Eurema laeta*	N/A	
Chocolate Grass Yellow	*Eurema sari*	N/A	
The Philippine Chocolate Grass Yellow	*Eurema sarilata*	N/A	Endemic
Changeable Grass Yellow	*Eurema simulatrix*	N/A	
Tree Yellow	*Gandaca harina*	N/A	
Common Forest White	*Appias aegis*	EN	
White Albatross	*Appias albina*	N/A	
Plain Puffin	*Appias indra*	N/A	
Chocolate albatross	*Appias lyncida*	N/A	
Maria Albatross	*Appias maria*	N/A	Endemic
Dark Yellow Albatross	*Appias nephele*	N/A	
Orange Albatross	*Appias nero*	N/A	
Striped Albatross	*Appias olferna*	N/A	
Yellow Albatross	*Appias paulina*	N/A	
Banded Puffin	*Appias phoebe*	N/A	Endemic
Panay Puffin	*Appias remedios*	N/A	Endemic
Palawan Puffin	*Appias waltraudae*	N/A	Endemic
Orange Gull	*Cepora aspasia*	N/A	
Philippine Gull	*Cepora boisduvaliana*	N/A	Endemic
Apo Jezebel	*Delias apoensis*	N/A	Endemic
Baracasa Jezebel	*Delias baracasa*	N/A	
Blanca Jezebel	*Delias blanca*	VU	
Black Jezebel	*Delias diaphana*	N/A	Endemic
Ganymedes Jezebel	*Delias ganymedes*	N/A	Endemic
Georgina Jezebel	*Delias georgina*	N/A	
Common Jezebel	*Delias henningia*	N/A	
Mindoro Jezebel	*Delias hidecoae*	LR-cd	Endemic
Painted Jezebel	*Delias hyparete*	VU	
Levicki's Jezebel	*Delias levicki*	VU	Endemic
Magsadana's Jezebel	*Delias magsadana*	VU	Endemic
Nuyda Jezebel	*Delias nuydaorum*	N/A	Endemic
Ottonia Jezebel	*Delias ottonia*	N/A	Endemic
Luzon Jezebel	*Delias paoaiensis*	N/A	Endemic
Red-Based Jezebel	*Delias pasithoe*	LR-cd	
Schoenig's Jezebel	*Delias schoenigi*	N/A	Endemic
Lion Jezebel	*Delias singhapura*	N/A	
The Yellow Jezebel	*Delias themis*	N/A	Endemic

Common Names	Scientific Names	Status	Endemicity
Wood's Jezebel	*Delias woodi*	N/A	Endemic
Great Orange Tip	*Hebomoia glaucippe*	N/A	
The Philippine Orange-Tip	*Ixias clarki*	EX?	Endemic
Psyche	*Leptosia nina*	N/A	
Philippine Wanderer	*Pareronia boebera*	N/A	Endemic
Gulussa Wanderer	*Pareronia gulussa*	N/A	
Palawan Wanderer	*Pareronia nishiyamai*	N/A	Endemic
Mindanao Wanderer	*Pareronia phocaea*	N/A	Endemic
Malayan Wanderer	*Pareronia valeria*	N/A	
Cabbage White	*Pieris canidia*	N/A	
Malaysian Albatross	*Saletara panda*	N/A	
Forest White	*Udaiana cynis*	N/A	
NYMPHALIDAE (Brushfoots, Sergeants & Satyrs)			
Philippine Rajah	*Charaxes amycus*	N/A	Endemic
Mindanao Rajah	*Charaxes antonius*	N/A	Endemic
Tawny Rajah	*Charaxes bajula*	N/A	Endemic
Palawan Rajah	*Charaxes bupalus*	N/A	Endemic
Double Eye-spotted Rajah	*Charaxes harmodius*	N/A	
Platen's Rajah	*Charaxes plateni*	N/A	Endemic
Southern Rajah	*Charaxes sangana*	VU; CR	Endemic
Black Rajah	*Charaxes solon*	N/A	
Common Nawab	*Polyura athamas*	N/A	
Jewelled Nawab	*Polyura delphis*	N/A	
Malayan Yellow Nawab	*Polyura moori*	N/A	
Blue Nawab	*Polyura schreiber*	LR-cd	
Begum	*Agatasa chrysodonia*	LR-cd; VU	Endemic
Blue Begum	*Prothoe franck*	N/A	
Semper's Begum	*Prothoe semperi*	N/A	Endemic
Platen's Begum	*Prothoe plateni*	N/A	Endemic
Malay Tiger	*Danaus affinis*	N/A	
Plain Tiger	*Danaus chrysippus*	N/A	
Common Tiger	*Danaus genutia*	N/A	
White Tiger	*Danaus melanippus*	N/A	
Smaller Wood Nymph	*Ideopsis gaura*	N/A	
Grey Glassy Tiger	*Ideopsis juventa*	N/A	
Dark Blue Glassy Tiger	*Ideopsis vulgaris*	N/A	
Yellow Glassy Tiger	*Parantica aspasia*	N/A	
Dannatt's Tiger	*Parantica dannatti*	VU	Endemic
David's Tiger	*Parantica davidi*	VU	Endemic
Luzon Glassy Tiger	*Parantica luzonensis*	N/A	
Milagros' Tiger	*Parantica milagros*	EN	Endemic
Noel's Tiger	*Parantica noeli*	VU	Endemic
Felder's Tiger	*Parantica phyle*	VU	Endemic
Father Schoenig's Chocolate Tiger	*Parantica schoenigi*	VU	Endemic
Chestnut Tiger	*Parantica sita*	N/A	
Glassy Tiger	*Parantica vitrina*	LC	Endemic
Dark Blue Tiger	*Tirumala hamata*	N/A	
Blue Tiger	*Tirumala ishmoides*	N/A	
Broad Blue Tiger	*Tirumala limniace*	N/A	
Narrow Dark Blue Tiger	*Tirumala septentrionis*	N/A	
Mindanao Blue Tiger	*Tirumala tumanana*	VU	Endemic
Long-branded Blue Crow	*Euploea algea*	N/A	
Schaus' Crow	*Euploea blossomae*	NT	Endemic
Blue King Crow	*Euploea camaralzeman*	N/A	
Spotted Black Crow	*Euploea crameri*	N/A	
Blue-Branded King Crow	*Euploea eunice*	N/A	
The Lesser Striped Blue Crow	*Euploea eyndhovii*	N/A	
Blue-Spotted Crow	*Euploea midamus*	N/A	
Striped Blue Crow	*Euploea mulciber*	N/A	
The Giant Crow	*Euploea phaenareta*	N/A	

Common Names	Scientific Names	Status	Endemicity
Swainson's Crow	Euploea swainson	NT	
Double-Branded Crow	Euploea sylvester	N/A	
Tobler's Crow	Euploea tobleri	NT	Endemic
Dwarf CROW	Euploea tulliolus	N/A	
Electra's Tree Nymph	Idea electra	VU	Endemic
Paper Kite	Idea leuconoe	N/A	
Common Tree Nymph	Idea stolli	VU	
Blue Beak	Libythea geoffroy	N/A	
Club Beak	Libythea myrrha	N/A	
White-Spotted Beak	Libythea narina	N/A	
Common Palmking	Amathusia phidippus	N/A	
Koh-I-Noor	Amathuxidia amythaon	VU	
Dodong's Duffer	Discophora dodong	N/A	Endemic
Blue Duffer	Discophora necho	N/A	
Purple Duffer	Discophora ogina	N/A	Endemic
Purple-spotted Duffer	Discophora philippina	N/A	Endemic
Lesser Purple Duffer	Discophora simplex	LR-cd	
Common Duffer	Discophora sondaica	VU	
Common Faun	Faunis phaon	N/A	Endemic
White Banded Faun	Faunis sappho	N/A	Endemic
Pale Banded Faun	Faunis stomphax	N/A	
Silky Owl	Taenaris horsfieldii	N/A	
Common Saturn	Zeuxidia amethystus	N/A	
Semper's Saturn	Zeuxidia semperi	VU	Endemic
Broad Purple Saturn	Zeuxidia sibulana	N/A	Endemic
Courtesan	Euripus nyctelius	N/A	
Luzon Emperor	Helcyra miyazakii	CR	Endemic
Philippine Circe	Hestinalis dissimilis	N/A	Endemic
Mindanao Circe	Hestinalis waterstradti	N/A	Endemic
Black Prince	Rohana parisatis	N/A	
Luzon Prince	Rohana rhea	N/A	
Common Castor	Ariadne merione	N/A	
Philippine Castor	Ariadne taeniata	N/A	Endemic
Blue Dandy	Laringa castelnaui	N/A	
Intermediate Maplet	Chersonesia intermedia	N/A	
Rounded Maplet	Chersonesia peraka	N/A	
Wavy maplet	Chersonesia rahria	N/A	
Cassander Mapwing	Cyrestis cassander	N/A	Endemic
Dark-lined Mapwing	Cyrestis kudrati	N/A	Endemic
Common Mapwing	Cyrestis maenalis	N/A	
Straight-lined Mapwing	Cyrestis nivea	N/A	
Little Banded Yeoman	Algia fasciata	N/A	
Laced Fritillary	Argyreus hyperbius	N/A	
Red Lacewing	Cethosia biblis	N/A	
Malay Lacewing	Cethosia hypsea	N/A	
Luzon Lacewing	Cethosia luzonica	N/A	Endemic
Mindanao Lacewing	Cethosia mindanensis	N/A	Endemic
Yeoman	Cirrochroa menones	N/A	Endemic
Satellite Yeoman	Cirrochroa satellita	N/A	
Common Yeoman	Cirrochroa tyche	N/A	
Common Rustic	Cupha arias	N/A	
Rustic	Cupha erymanthis	N/A	
Small Leopard	Phalanta alcippe	N/A	
Common Leopard	Phalanta phalantha	N/A	
Malayan Assyrian	Terinos ciarissa	N/A	
Philippine Assyrian	Terinos romeo	VU	Endemic
Vagrant	Vagrans sinha	N/A	
Malayan Cruiser	Vindula dejone	N/A	
Common Cruiser	Vindula erota	N/A	
Autumn Leaf	Doleschallia bisaltide	N/A	

Common Names	Scientific Names	Status	Endemicity
Malayan Eggfly	Hypolimnas anomala	N/A	
Great Eggfly	Hypolimnas bolina	N/A	
Danaid Eggfly	Hypolimnas misippus	N/A	
Peacock Pansy	Junonia almana	N/A	
Grey Pansy	Junonia atlites	N/A	
Brown Pansy	Junonia hedonia	N/A	
Chocolate Pansy	Junonia iphita	N/A	
Lemon Pansy	Junonia lemonias	N/A	
Blue Pansy	Junonia orithya	N/A	
Blue Admiral	Kaniska canace	N/A	
Wizard	Rhinopalpa polynice	N/A	
Common Jester	Symbrenthia hippoclus	N/A	
Intricate Jester	Symbrenthia hypatia	N/A	
Himalayan Jester	Symbrenthia hypselis	N/A	
Common Jester	Symbrenthia lilaea	N/A	
Painted Lady	Vanessa cardui	N/A	
Dejeani Painted Lady	Vanessa dejeani	N/A	
Indian Red Admiral	Vanessa indica	N/A	
Lurcher	Yoma sabina	N/A	
Constable	Dichorragia nesimachus	N/A	
Typical Sergeant	Athyma alcamene	N/A	Endemic
Luzon Sergeant	Athyma arayata	N/A	Endemic
Studded Sergeant	Athyma asura	N/A	
Godmani Sergeant	Athyma godmani	N/A	Endemic
Kasa Sergeant	Athyma kasa	N/A	Endemic
Philipppine Sergeant	Athyma maenas	N/A	Endemic
Mindanao Sergeant	Athyma mindanica	N/A	Endemic
Colour Sergeant	Athyma nefte	N/A	
Dinagat Sergeant	Athyma obsoleta	N/A	Endemic
Common Sergeant	Athyma perius	N/A	
Lance Sergeant	Athyma pravara	EN	
Malay Staff Sergeant	Athyma reta	EN	
Palawan Sergeant	Athyma salvini	N/A	Endemic
Saski Sergeant	Athyma saskia	VU	Endemic
Staff Sergeant	Athyma selenophora	N/A	
Separate Sergeant	Athyma separata	N/A	Endemic
Special Sergeant	Athyma speciosa	N/A	Endemic
Venata Sergeant	Athyma venata	N/A	Endemic
Great Marquis	Bassarona dunya	N/A	
Philippine Marquis	Bassarona piratica	VU	Endemic
Redtail Marquis	Bassarona recta	N/A	
Banded Marquis	Bassarona teuta	N/A	
Horsfield's Baron	Cynitia cocytina	N/A	
Godart's Baron	Cynitia godartii	VU	
Fruhstorfer's Baron	Cynitia phlegethon	N/A	Endemic
Semper's Baron	Cynitia semperi	N/A	Endemic
Redspot Duke	Dophla evelina	N/A	
Mango Baron	Euthalia aconthea	N/A	
Green Baron	Euthalia adonia	N/A	
Streaked Baron	Euthalia alpheda	N/A	
Grey Baron	Euthalia anosia	EN	
Red-Spot Baron	Euthalia djata	N/A	
Common Gaudy Baron	Euthalia lubentina	N/A	
Philippine Baron	Euthalia lusiada	N/A	Endemic
Blue Baron	Euthalia mahadeva	N/A	
Mindanao Baron	Euthalia mindanaensis	VU	Endemic
Malay Baron	Euthalia monina	N/A	
Palawan Baron	Euthalia tanagra	N/A	Endemic
Bella Sailer	Lasippa bella	N/A	Endemic
Ebusa Sailer	Lasippa ebusa	N/A	Endemic

Common Names	Scientific Names	Status	Endemicity
Illigera Sailer	Lasippa illigera	N/A	Endemic
Palawan Sailer	Lasippa illigerella	N/A	Endemic
Tiger Lascar	Lasippa monata	N/A	
Pata Sailer	Lasippa pata	N/A	Endemic
Bohol Sailer	Lasippa pizarrasi	VU	Endemic
The Knight	Lebadea martha	N/A	
The Yellow Archduke	Lexias canescens	N/A	
The Black Archduke	Lexias damalis	N/A	Endemic
Black-Tip Archduke	Lexias dirtea	N/A	
Luzon Archduke	Lexias hikarugenzi	N/A	Endemic
Orange Archduke	Lexias panopus	N/A	Endemic
Yellow-Tip Archduke	Lexias pardalis	N/A	
Mountain Blue Archduke	Lexias satrapes	N/A	Endemic
Visayan Commander	Moduza jumaloni	N/A	Endemic
Mata Commander	Moduza mata	N/A	Endemic
Nuyda Commander	Moduza nuydai	N/A	Endemic
Pintuyana Commander	Moduza pintuyana	N/A	Endemic
Common Commander	Moduza procris	N/A	
Thespias Commander	Moduza thespias	N/A	Endemic
Urdaneta Commander	Moduza urdaneta	N/A	Endemic
The Rich Sailer	Neptis anjana	N/A	
Clear Sailor	Neptis clinia	N/A	
Cymela Commander	Neptis cymela	N/A	Endemic
Cyra Commander	Neptis cyra	N/A	Endemic
Malayan Sailor	Neptis duryodana	N/A	
Felisimilis Sailor	Neptis felisimilis	VU	Endemic
Dingiest Sailor	Neptis harita	N/A	
Common Sailor	Neptis hylas	N/A	
Typical Sailer	Neptis mindorana	N/A	Endemic
Omeroda Sailer	Neptis omeroda	N/A	
Pampanga Commander	Neptis pampanga	N/A	Endemic
Sunica Commander	Neptis sunica	N/A	Endemic
Colonel	Pandita sinope	N/A	
Lascar	Pantoporia cyrilla	N/A	Endemic
Dama Lascar	Pantoporia dama	N/A	Endemic
Epira Lascar	Pantoporia epira	EX?; VU	Endemic
Common Lascar	Pantoporia hordonia	VU	
Perak Lascar	Pantoporia paraka	N/A	
Clipper	Parthenos sylvia	N/A	
Short-Banded Gray Sailor	Phaedyma columella	N/A	
Sergeant	Tacola larymna	N/A	
Magindana Commander	Tacola magindana	N/A	Endemic
Short-Banded Viscount	Tanaecia aruna	N/A	
Calliphorus Viscount	Tanaecia calliphorus	N/A	Endemic
Dodong Viscount	Tanaecia dodong	CR	Endemic
Leucotaenia Viscount	Tanaecia leucotaenia	N/A	Endemic
Lupina Viscount	Tanaecia lupina	CR	Endemic
Pelea Viscount	Tanaecia pelea	N/A	
Susoni Viscount	Tanaecia susoni	CR	Endemic
Cosmia Commander	Tarattia cosmia	N/A	Endemic
Gutama Sergeant	Tarattia gutama	N/A	Endemic
Mindanao Pale Ringlet	Acrophtalmia albofasciata	N/A	Endemic
Artemis Pale Ringlet	Acrophtalmia artemis	N/A	Endemic
Leto Pale Ringlet	Acrophtalmia leto	N/A	Endemic
Luzon Pale Ringlet	Acrophtalmia luzonica	N/A	Endemic
Negros Pale Ringlet	Acrophtalmia yamashitai	N/A	Endemic
Bisaya Bushbrown	Culapa bisaya	N/A	Endemic
Tagala Bushbrown	Culapa tagala	N/A	Endemic
Beza Palmfly	Elymnias beza	N/A	Endemic
Casiphonides Palmfly	Elymnias casiphonides	N/A	Endemic

Common Names	Scientific Names	Status	Endemicity
Congruens Palmfly	Elymnias congruens	N/A	Endemic
White-Banded Palmfly	Elymnias dara	N/A	
Green Palmfly	Elymnias esaca	N/A	
Kanekoi Palmfly	Elymnias kanekoi	N/A	Endemic
Kochi Palmfly	Elymnias kochi	N/A	Endemic
Mindanao Palmfly	Elymnias luteofasciata	VU	Endemic
Melias Palmfly	Elymnias melias	N/A	Endemic
Tiger Palmfly	Elymnias nesaea	N/A	
Tawny Palmfly	Elymnias panthera	N/A	
Parce Palmfly	Elymnias parce	N/A	Endemic
Sansoni Palmfly	Elymnias sansoni	N/A	Endemic
Eyed Cyclops	Erites argentina	N/A	
Angle Red Forester	Lethe chandica	N/A	
Bamboo Treebrown	Lethe europa	N/A	
Evening Brown	Melanitis atrax	N/A	Endemic
Forest Evening Brown	Melanitis boisduvalia	N/A	
Common Evening Brown	Melanitis leda	N/A	
Great Evening Brown	Melanitis zitenius	N/A	
Aramis Bushbrown	Mycalesis aramis	N/A	Endemic
Frederici Bushbrown	Mycalesis frederici	N/A	Endemic
Georgi Bushbrown	Mycalesis georgi	N/A	Endemic
Horsfield's Bushbrown	Mycalesis horsfieldi	N/A	
Igoleta Bushbrown	Mycalesis igoleta	N/A	Endemic
Janardana Bush Brown	Mycalesis janardana	N/A	
Kashiwai Bushbrown	Mycalesis kashiwaii	N/A	Endemic
Kurosawai Bushbrown	Mycalesis kurosawai	N/A	Endemic
Dark-Branded Bushbrown	Mycalesis mineus	N/A	
Purple Bushbrown	Mycalesis orseis	N/A	
Common Bushbrown	Mycalesis perseus	N/A	
Tamaraw Bushbrown	Mycalesis tamarau	N/A	Endemic
Felder's Bushbrown	Mydosama felderi	N/A	Endemic
Ita Bushbrown	Mydosama ita	N/A	Endemic
Teatus Bushbrown	Mydosama teatus	N/A	Endemic
Treadaway's Bushbrown	Mydosama treadawayi	N/A	Endemic
Malayan Owl	Neorina lowii	N/A	
Dark Grass Brown Or Medus Brown	Orsotriaena medus	N/A	
Common Satyr	Ptychandra leucogyne	N/A	Endemic
Lorquin's Satyr	Ptychandra lorquinii	N/A	Endemic
Mindoro Satyr	Ptychandra mindorana	N/A	Endemic
Negros Satyr	Ptychandra negrosensis	N/A	Endemic
Ohtani Satyr	Ptychandra ohtanii	LR-cd	Endemic
Schadenberg Satyr	Ptychandra schadenbergi	N/A	Endemic
Leyte Striped Ringlet	Ragadia crohonica	N/A	Endemic
Luzon Striped Ringlet	Ragadia luzonia	N/A	Endemic
Palawan Striped Ringlet	Ragadia maganda	N/A	Endemic
Mindanao Striped Ringlet	Ragadia melindena	N/A	Endemic
Mindoro Striped Ringlet	Ragadia mindorana	N/A	Endemic
Tsukada Striped Ringlet	Ragadia tsukadai	N/A	Endemic
Common Three-Ring	Ypthima baldus	N/A	
Burmese Three-Ring	Ypthima norma	N/A	
Common Three-Ring	Ypthima sempera	N/A	Endemic
Mindanao Three-Ring	Ypthima sensilis	N/A	Endemic
Common Five-Ring	Ypthima stellera	N/A	Endemic
Mindanao Wallacean	Zethera hestioides	N/A	Endemic
Southern Wallacean	Zethera musa	N/A	Endemic
Central Wallacean	Zethera musides	N/A	Endemic
Northern Wallacean	Zethera pimplea	N/A	Endemic
Eastern Wallacean	Zethera thermaea	N/A	Endemic
Data Treebrown	Zophoessa dataensis	N/A	Endemic

Common Names	Scientific Names	Status	Endemicity
LYCAENIDAE (Blues, Harvesters & Hairstreaks)			
Pale Sunbeam	Curetis nesophila	N/A	
Sunbeam	Curetis tagalica	N/A	
The Moth Butterfly	Liphyra brassolis	EN;VU	
Club Silverline	Cigaritis negrita	N/A	
Common Hedge Blue	Acytolepis puspa	N/A	
Common Ciliate Blue	Anthene emolus	N/A	
The White Ciliate Blue	Anthene licates	N/A	
Pointed Ciliate Blue	Anthene lycaenina	N/A	
Pierrot	Caleta argola	N/A	
Elbowed Pierrot	Caleta elna	N/A	
Straight Pierrot	Caleta roxus	N/A	
The Philippine Hedge Blue	Callenya kaguya	N/A	Endemic
Common Pierrot	Castalius rosimon	N/A	
Ancyra Blue/ Felder's Lineblue	Catopyrops ancyra	N/A	
Silver Forget-Me-Not	Catochrysops panormus	N/A	
Forget-Me-Not	Catochrysops strabo	N/A	
Penelope's Hedge-Blue	Cebrella penelope	N/A	Endemic
Southern Hedge Blue	Celarchus archagathos	N/A	Endemic
Hermarchus Hedge Blue	Celarchus hermarchus	N/A	Endemic
Algernoni Hedge Blue	Celastrina algernoni	N/A	
Holly Blue	Celastrina argiolus	N/A	
Plain Hedge Blue	Celastrina lavendularis	N/A	
Philippine Hedge Blue	Celastrina philippina	N/A	
Lime Blue	Chilades lajus	N/A	
Mindoro Cupid	Chilades mindora	N/A	Endemic
Plains Cupid	Chilades pandava	N/A	
Banded Blue Pierrot	Discolampa ulysses	N/A	
Gram Blue	Euchrysops cnejus	N/A	
Indian Cupid	Everes lacturnus	N/A	
Black-spotted Grass Blue	Famegana alsulus	N/A	
Grass Jewel	Freyeria putli	N/A	
Pointed Line Blue	Ionolyce helicon	N/A	
Metallic Cerulean	Jamides alecto	N/A	
Alsietus Cerulean	Jamides alsietus	N/A	
Aratus Cerulean	Jamides aratus	N/A	
Dark Cerulean	Jamides bochus	N/A	
Callistus Cerulean	Jamides callistus	N/A	
Camarines Cerulean	Jamides camarines	N/A	Endemic
Common Cerulean	Jamides celeno	N/A	
Pale White Cerulean	Jamides cleodus	N/A	
Pale Cerulean	Jamides cyta	N/A	
Glistening Cerulean	Jamides elpis	N/A	
Espada Cerulean	Jamides espada	N/A	
Burmese Cerulean	Jamides philatus	N/A	
White Cerulean	Jamides pura	N/A	
Schatzi Cerulean	Jamides schatzi	N/A	
Seki Cerulean	Jamides sekii	N/A	Endemic
Suidas Cerulean	Jamides suidas	N/A	
Peablue	Lampides boeticus	N/A	
Zebra Blue	Leptotes plinius	N/A	
Yoshida Hedge Blue	Lestranicus yoshidai	N/A	Endemic
Malayan	Megisba malaya	N/A	
Apo Hedge Blue	Monodontides apona	N/A	Endemic
Honda Hedge Blue	Monodontides hondai	N/A	Endemic
Kolari Hedge Blue	Monodontides kolari	N/A	
Luzon Hedge Blue	Monodontides luzonensis	N/A	Endemic
White Lineblue	Nacaduba angusta	N/A	
Rounded Six-Line Blue	Nacaduba berenice	N/A	
Opaque Six-Line Blue	Nacaduba beroe	N/A	

Common Names	Scientific Names	Status	Endemicity
Pale Four-Line Blue	Nacaduba hermus	N/A	
Transparent Six-Line Blue	Nacaduba kurava	N/A	
Limbura Lineblue	Nacaduba limbura	N/A	Endemic
Metallic Lineblue	Nacaduba metallica	N/A	
Neaira Lineblue	Nacaduba neaira	N/A	Endemic
Small Four-Line Blue	Nacaduba pavana	N/A	
Jewel Fourline Blue	Nacaduba sanaya	N/A	
The White Lineblue	Nacaduba sericina	N/A	Endemic
Four-Line Blue	Nacaduba subperusia	N/A	
Quaker	Neopithecops iolanthe	N/A	
Common Quaker	Neopithecops zalmora	N/A	
Mindanao Pierrot	Niphanda anthenoides	N/A	Endemic
Large Pointed Pierrot	Niphanda tessellata	N/A	
Dark Green-banded Blue	Nothodanis schaeffera	N/A	
Dingy LineBlue	Petrelaea dana	N/A	
Mauve Lineblue	Petrelaea tombugensis	N/A	
Forest Quaker	Pithecops corvus	N/A	
Banded Lineblue	Prosotas aluta	N/A	
Tail-Less Lineblue	Prosotas dubiosa	N/A	
Dark-based Lineblue	Prosotas gracilis	N/A	
Maputi Lineblue	Prosotas maputi	VU	Endemic
Nelides Lineblue	Prosotas nelides	N/A	
Common Line Blue	Prosotas nora	N/A	
Pale Grass Blue	Pseudozizeeria maha	N/A	
Murayama Hedge Blue	Sidima murayamai	VU	Endemic
Separate Pierrot	Tarucus waterstradti	EN	
Aemulus Hedge Blue	Udara aemulus	VU	Endemic
Camenae Hedge Blue	Udara camenae	N/A	
Cyma Hedge Blue	Udara cyma	N/A	
Pale Hedge Blue	Udara dilecta	N/A	
Dilectissima Hedge Blue	Udara dilectissima	N/A	
Nishiyama Hedge Blue	Udara nishiyamai	N/A	Endemic
Narrow-Bordered Hedge Blue	Udara placidula	N/A	
Rona Hedge Blue	Udara rona	N/A	
Santo Hedge Blue	Udara santotomasana	N/A	Endemic
Bicoloured Hedge Blue	Udara selma	N/A	
Tyotaroi Hedge Blue	Udara tyotaroi	N/A	Endemic
Wileman Hedge Blue	Udara wilemani	N/A	Endemic
Philippine Singleton	Una philippensis	VU	Endemic
Dark Grass Blue	Zizeeria karsandra	N/A	
Lesser Grass Blue	Zizina otis	N/A	
Tiny Grass Blue	Zizula hylax	N/A	
Mindanao Tinsel	Acupicta inopinatum	CR	Endemic
Leaf Blue	Amblypodia narada	N/A	
Silver Royal	Ancema blanka	N/A	
Witch	Araotes lapithis	N/A	
Philippine Witch	Araotes perrhaebis	VU	Endemic
Aberrant Oakblue	Arhopala abseus	N/A	
Large Metallic Oakblue	Arhopala aedias	N/A	
Purple-glazed Oakblue	Arhopala agaba	N/A	Endemic
Agesias Oakblue	Arhopala agesias	N/A	
Corbet Dull Oakblue	Arhopala agesilaus	N/A	
Niceville's Oakblue	Arhopala agrata	N/A	
Patchy Oakblue	Arhopala alaconia	N/A	
Pallid Oakblue	Arhopala alesia	N/A	
Alexandrae's Oakblue	Arhopala alexandrae	N/A	Endemic
Purple Broken-Band Oakblue	Arhopala alitaeus	N/A	
Rosy Oakblue	Arhopala allata	N/A	
Broad Yellow Oakblue	Arhopala amphimuta	N/A	
Anamuta Oakblue	Arhopala anamuta	N/A	Endemic

Common Names	Scientific Names	Status	Endemicity
Annulata Oakblue	*Arhopala annulata*	N/A	
Magnificent Oakblue	*Arhopala anthelus*	N/A	
Deep-purple Oakblue	*Arhopala aroa*	N/A	
Lined Oakblue	*Arhopala aronya*	N/A	Endemic
Arsenius Oakblue	*Arhopala arsenius*	VU	Endemic
Vinous Oakblue	*Arhopala athada*	N/A	
Tailed Disc Oakblue	*Arhopala atosia*	N/A	
Niceville's Dull Oakblue	*Arhopala avatha*	N/A	
Barbarus Oakblue	*Arhopala barbarus*	N/A	Endemic
Burmese Bushblue	*Arhopala birmana*	N/A	
Buddha Oakblue	*Arhopala buddha*	N/A	
Powdered Oakblue	*Arhopala bazalus*	N/A	
Calayan Oakblue	*Arhopala calayana*	N/A	Endemic
Centaur Oakkblue	*Arhopala centaurus*	N/A	
Chameleon Oakblue	*Arhopala chamaeleona*	N/A	
Large Mergui Oakblue	*Arhopala cleander*	N/A	
Ultramarine Oakblue	*Arhopala corinda*	N/A	
Davao Oakblue	*Arhopala davaona*	N/A	Endemic
Detrita Oakblue	*Arhopala detrita*	N/A	Endemic
Violetdisc Oakblue	*Arhopala epimete*	N/A	
Eridanus Oakblue	*Arhopala eridanus*	N/A	
Green Oakblue	*Arhopala eumolphus*	N/A	
Kalimantan Oakblue	*Arhopala evansi*	N/A	
Spotless Oakblue	*Arhopala fulla*	N/A	
Grand Oakblue	*Arhopala grandimuta*	N/A	Endemic
Hayashi Oakblue	*Arhopala hayashihisakazui*	N/A	
Hesba Oakblue	*Arhopala hesba*	N/A	Endemic
Beloved Oakblue	*Arhopala hinigugma*	N/A	Endemic
Peacock Oakblue	*Arhopala horsfieldi*	N/A	
Ilocana Oakblue	*Arhopala ilocana*	LR-cd	Endemic
Brown Tornal Oakblue	*Arhopala inornata*	N/A	
Lesser Disc Oakblue	*Arhopala lurida*	N/A	
Luzon Oakblue	*Arhopala luzonensis*	VU	Endemic
Major Yellow Oakblue	*Arhopala major*	N/A	
Matsutaroi Oakblue	*Arhopala matsutaroi*	N/A	Endemic
Mindanao Oakblue	*Arhopala mindanaensis*	N/A	Endemic
Myrtha Oakblue	*Arhopala myrtha*	N/A	Endemic
Malayan Oakblue	*Arhopala myrzala*	N/A	
Ocrida Oakblue	*Arhopala ocrida*	N/A	Endemic
Dusky Bushblue	*Arhopala paraganesa*	N/A	
Sumatran Oakblue	*Arhopala phaenops*	N/A	
Pseudovihara Oakblue	*Arhopala pseudovihara*	N/A	Endemic
Rudepoema Oakblue	*Arhopala rudepoema*	N/A	Endemic
Sakaguchii Oakblue	*Arhopala sakaguchii*	N/A	Endemic
Reddish-brown Oakblue	*Arhopala selta*	N/A	
Shigae Oakblue	*Arhopala shigae*	N/A	Endemic
Sylhet Oakblue	*Arhopala silhetensis*	N/A	
Simon Oakblue	*Arhopala simoni*	VU	Endemic
Staudinger's Oakblue	*Arhopala staudingeri*	N/A	Endemic
Tephlis Oakblue	*Arhopala tephlis*	N/A	
Theba Oakblue	*Arhopala theba*	N/A	Endemic
Tindongan's Oakblue	*Arhopala tindongani*	EN	Endemic
Tomokoae Oakblue	*Arhopala tomokoae*	N/A	Endemic
Trionoea Oakblue	*Arhopala trionoea*	N/A	Endemic
Zambra Oakblue	*Arhopala zambra*	N/A	
N/A	*Austrozephyrus reginae*	N/A	Endemic
Plane	*Bindahara phocides*	N/A	
Evan's Tinsel	*Catapaecilma evansi*	LR-cd	
Gracilis Tinsel	*Catapaecilma gracilis*	N/A	Endemic
Nakamoto Tinsel	*Catapaecilma nakamotoi*	LR-cd	Endemic

Common Names	Scientific Names	Status	Endemicity
Green Imperial	Manto hypoleuca	N/A	
Blue Royal	Matsutaroa iljai	N/A	Endemic
Manata Hairstreak	Neocheritra manata	VU	Endemic
Annie's Royal	Paruparo annie	VU	Endemic
Cebu Royal	Paruparo cebuensis	N/A	Endemic
Lumawig Royal	Paruparo lumawigi	N/A	Endemic
Mamertina Royal	Paruparo mamertina	N/A	Endemic
Southern Royal	Paruparo mio	N/A	Endemic
Rosemarie Royal	Paruparo rosemarie	VU	Endemic
Violacea Royal	Paruparo violacea	VU	Endemic
White Tufted Royal	Pratapa deva	N/A	
Smoky Blue Royal	Pratapa icetoides	N/A	
Tyotaroi Royal	Pratapa tyotaroi	VU; LR-cd	Endemic
Dawnas Royal	Pseudotajuria donatana	N/A	
Australis Royal	Rachana australis	VU	Endemic
Circumdata Royal	Rachana circumdata	N/A	Endemic
Banded Royal	Rachana jalindra	VU;EN;LR-cd	
Mariaba Royal	Rachana mariaba	N/A	Endemic
Mioae Royal	Rachana mioae	N/A	Endemic
Platen's Royal	Rachana plateni	EN	Endemic
Flash	Rapala caerulescens	N/A	
Damona Flash	Rapala damona	N/A	Endemic
Scarlet Flash	Rapala dieneces	N/A	
Diopites Flash	Rapala diopites	N/A	Endemic
Elcia Flash	Rapala elcia	N/A	Endemic
Myanmar Flash	Rapala hades	N/A	
Slate Flash	Rapala manea	N/A	
Masara Flash	Rapala masara	LR-cd	Endemic
Fruhstorfer's Flash	Rapala melida	N/A	
Scarce Shot Blue	Rapala scintilla	N/A	
Tomokoae Flash	Rapala tomokoae	N/A	Endemic
Indigo Flash	Rapala varuna	N/A	
Zamona Flash	Rapala zamona	N/A	Endemic
Davis Royal	Remelana davisi	N/A	Endemic
Chocolate Royal	Remelana jangala	N/A	
Philippine Chocolate Royal	Remelana westermannii	N/A	Endemic
Orange Imperial	Ritra aurea	N/A	
Red-edge	Semanga superba	N/A	
Palawan Spark	Sinthusa kawazoei	N/A	Endemic
Mindanao Spark	Sinthusa mindanensis	N/A	Endemic
Narrow Spark	Sinthusa nasaka	N/A	
Philippine Spark	Sinthusa natsumiae	N/A	Endemic
Peregrin Spark	Sinthusa peregrinus	N/A	Endemic
Stephani's Spark	Sinthusa stephaniae	N/A	Endemic
Red Imperial	Suasa lisides liris	N/A	
Philippine Acacia Blue	Surendra manilana	N/A	Endemic
Green-scaled Acacia Blue	Surendra vivarna	N/A	
Mindoro Royal	Tajuria alangani	N/A	Endemic
Berenis Royal	Tajuria berenis	N/A	
Flash Royal	Tajuria deudorix	N/A	Endemic
Dominus Royal	Tajuria dominus	N/A	Endemic
Igolatiana Royal	Tajuria igolotiana	N/A	Endemic
Bornean Royal	Tajuria isaeus	N/A	
Pale Blue Royal	Tajuria jalajala	N/A	Endemic
Felder's Royal	Tajuria mantra	N/A	
Hayashi's Royal	Tajuria matsutaroi	N/A	Endemic
Whiteline Guava Blue	Virachola kessuma	N/A	
Mindanao Guava Blue	Virachola masamichii	VU	Endemic
The Scarce Guava Blue	Virachola smilis	N/A	
Fluffy Tit	Hypolycaena amasa	N/A	

Common Names	Scientific Names	Status	Endemicity
Common Darkie	Allotinus albatus	N/A	
Apo Darkie	Allotinus albicans	N/A	Endemic
Apries Darkie	Allotinus apries	N/A	
Rounded Darkie	Allotinus corbeti	N/A	
White Darkie	Allotinus fallax	N/A	
Kudarat Darkie	Allotinus kudaratus	VU	Endemic
Luzon Darkie	Allotinus luzonensis	LR-cd	Endemic
Melos Darkie	Allotinus melos	N/A	
Mindanao Darkie	Allotinus nigritus	N/A	Endemic
Nivalis Darkie	Allotinus nivalis	N/A	
Semper's Darkie	Allotinus punctatus	LR-cd	Endemic
Samar Darkie	Allotinus samarensis	N/A	
Peninsular Darkie	Allotinus sarrastes	N/A	
Lesser Darkie	Allotinus substrigosus	N/A	
Blue Darkie	Allotinus subviolaceus	N/A	
Unicoloured Darkie	Allotinus unicolor	N/A	
Entire Mottle	Logania distanti	N/A	
Malayan Mottle	Logania malayica	N/A	
Pale Mottle	Logania marmorata	N/A	
Rounded Mottle	Logania regina	N/A	
Waltraud's Mottle	Logania waltraudae	VU	Endemic
N/A	Lontalius eltus	VU	
Atimonicus Brownie	Miletus atimonicus	LR-cd	Endemic
Basilan Brownie	Miletus bazilanus	N/A	Endemic
Brownie	Miletus drucei	N/A	
The Round-band Brownie	Miletus gopara	N/A	
Philippine Brownie	Miletus melanion	N/A	Endemic
Great Brownie	Miletus symethus	N/A	
Surigao Brownie	Miletus takanamii	VU	Endemic
Apefly	Spalgis epius	N/A	
Apo Apefly	Spalgis takanamii	LR-cd	Endemic
Forest Pierrot	Taraka hamada	N/A	
Emerald	Cyaniriodes libna	VU; EN	
Philippine Emerald	Cyaniriodes siraspiorum	N/A	Endemic
Bidotata Bluejohn	Deramas bidotata	N/A	Endemic
Evelyn Bluejhon	Deramas evelynae	N/A	Endemic
Ikedai Bluejohn	Deramas ikedai	LR-cd	Endemic
Manobo Bluejohn	Deramas manobo	N/A	Endemic
Mindanao Bluejohn	Deramas mindanensis	VU	Endemic
Montana Bluejohn	Deramas montana	N/A	Endemic
Rising Bluejohn	Deramas sumikat	VU	Endemic
Tomokoae Bluejohn	Deramas tomokoae	N/A	Endemic
Toshikoae Bluejohn	Deramas toshikoae	N/A	Endemic
Treadaway Bluejohn	Deramas treadawayi	N/A	Endemic
Philippine Gem	Poriskina phakos	VU	Endemic
Palawan Gem	Poritia kinoshitai	N/A	Endemic
Phama Gem	Poritia phama	N/A	
Malayan Gem	Poritia philota	N/A	
Borneo Gem	Poritia plateni	N/A	
Luzon Gem	Poritia solitaria	CR	Endemic
The Green-blue Brilliant	Simiskina pasira	N/A	
Broad-banded Brilliant	Simiskina phalena	N/A	
Blue Brilliant	Simiskina phalia	N/A	
RIODINIDAE (Metalmarks)			
Common Punchinello	Zemeros flegyas	N/A	
White Punch	Dodona deodata	N/A	
Larger Harlequin	Taxila haquinus	N/A	
Straight Plum Judy	Abisara kausambi	N/A	
Common Plum Judy	Abisara echerius	N/A	
Forest Judy	Abisara saturata	N/A	

Common Names	Scientific Names	Status	Endemicity
Major Ace	Halpe major	N/A	Endemic
Lesser Palawan Ace	Halpe palawea	N/A	Endemic
Negros Ace	Halpe purpurascens	N/A	Endemic
Suflur-Spotted Ace	Halpe sulphurifera	N/A	Endemic
Mindanao Ace	Halpe tilia	VU	Endemic
Palawan Ace	Halpe toxopea	N/A	
Coconut Skipper	Hidari irava	N/A	
Tree Flitter	Hyarotis adrastus	N/A	
Dark Tree Flitter	Hyarotis iadera	N/A	
Brush Tree Flitter	Hyarotis microsticta	N/A	
Narrow-winged Flitter	Isma binotatus	N/A	
The Lesser Long-spot Flitter	Isma bononia	N/A	
Broad White-spottted Flitter	Isma elioti	N/A	Endemic
Large Non-branded Flitter	Isma guttulifera	N/A	
Narrow-Banded Velvet Bob	Koruthaialos rubecula	N/A	
Shiny Velvet Bob	Koruthaialos sindu	N/A	
White-tipped Palmer	Lotongus calathus	N/A	
Common Redeye	Matapa aria	N/A	
Dark Yellow-fringed Redeye	Matapa celsina	N/A	
Fringed Redeye	Matapa cresta	N/A	
Lesser Yellow-fringed Redeye	Matapa intermedia	N/A	
The Banded Demon	Notocrypta clavata	N/A	
Restricted Demon	Notocrypta curvifascia	N/A	
Spotted Demon	Notocrypta feisthamelii	N/A	
Common Banded Demon	Notocrypta paralysos	N/A	
White Club Flitter	Oerane microthyrus	N/A	
Pale Dartlet	Oriens californica	N/A	Endemic
Black Dartlet	Oriens fons	N/A	Endemic
Common Dartlet	Oriens gola	N/A	
Oriental Straight Swift	Parnara bada	N/A	
Straight Swift	Parnara kawazoei	N/A	
Common Swift	Pelopidas agna	N/A	
The Conjoined Swift	Pelopidas conjuncta	N/A	
Small Branded Swift	Pelopidas mathias	N/A	
Brown Palmer	Pirdana fusca	VU	Endemic
Green-Striped Palmer	Pirdana hyela	N/A	
Silver-spot Lancer	Plastingia naga	N/A	
Yellow Chequered Lancer	Plastingia pellonia	N/A	
Orange Lancer	Plastingia viburnia	N/A	Endemic
Contiguous Swift	Polytremis lubricans	N/A	
Confucian Dart	Potanthus confucius	N/A	
Philippine Dartlet	Potanthus fettingi	N/A	
Ganda Dartlet	Potanthus ganda	N/A	
Large Dart	Potanthus hetaerus	N/A	
Hyuga Dartlet	Potanthus hyugai	N/A	Endemic
Zigzag Banded Dart	Potanthus mingo	N/A	
Mindanao Dartlet	Potanthus niobe	VU	Endemic
Lesser Dart	Potanthus omaha	N/A	
Yellow Band Dart	Potanthus pava	N/A	
Serina Dart	Potanthus serina	N/A	
Grass Skipper	Prusiana prusias	N/A	
Dusky Partwing	Psolos fuligo	N/A	
Agnesia Lancer	Pyroneura agnesia	N/A	
Spot-pointed Lancer	Pyroneura derna	N/A	
Lesser Lancer	Pyroneura flavia	N/A	
Philippine Lancer	Pyroneura liburnia	N/A	Endemic
Red Vein Lancer	Pyroneura niasana	N/A	
Mindanao Lancer	Pyroneura toshikoae	VU	Endemic
The Dubious Flitter	Quedara monteithi	N/A	
Purplish-grey Darter	Salanoemia fuscicornis	N/A	

Common Names	Scientific Names	Status	Endemicity
Multi-spotted Darter	*Salanoemia sala*	N/A	
Similar Sreak Darter	*Salanoemia similis*	N/A	
Grass Bob	*Suada albinus*	N/A	Endemic
Dark Grass Bob	*Suada catoleucos*	N/A	
Oriental Palm Bob	*Suastus gremius*	N/A	
Palm Bob	*Suastus migreus*	N/A	Endemic
Small Palm Bob	*Suastus minutus*	N/A	
Black Grass Dart	*Taractrocera ardonia*	N/A	
Luzon Grass Dart	*Taractrocera luzonensis*	N/A	
Dark Palm Dart	*Telicota ancilla*	N/A	
Bright-orange Darter	*Telicota augias*	N/A	
Common Palm Dart	*Telicota colon*	N/A	
Dark-dusted Palm Dart	*Telicota hilda*	N/A	
Narrow-branded Palm Dart	*Telicota ohara*	N/A	
Justin's Ace	*Thoressa justini*	VU	Endemic
Hoary Palmer	*Unkana ambasa*	N/A	
Grass Skipper	*Xanthoneura obscurior*	N/A	Endemic
Greenish Grass Skipper	*Xanthoneura telesinus*	N/A	Endemic
White-club Yellow Palmer	*Zela excellens*	N/A	
Pale-spotted Palmer	*Zela storeyi*	N/A	
Two-spot Palmer	*Zela zenon*	N/A	
Orange-Ciliate Palmer	*Zela zeus*	N/A	
Prominent Spot Flitter	*Zographetus doxus*	N/A	
Flitter	*Zographetus durga*	N/A	Endemic
Purple-Spotted Skipper	*Zographetus ogygia*	N/A	
Brown Flitter	*Zographetus pallens*	VU	Endemic
Small Flitter	*Zographetus rama*	N/A	
White-Banded Flat	*Celaenorrhinus asmara*	N/A	
Bazilanus Flat	*Celaenorrhinus bazilanus*	N/A	
Ficulnea Flat	*Celaenorrhinus ficulnea*	N/A	
Halcon Flat	*Celaenorrhinus halconis*	N/A	Endemic
Small Banded Flat	*Celaenorrhinus nigricans*	N/A	
Bengal Spotted Flat	*Celaenorrhinus putra*	N/A	
Spotted Flat	*Celaenorrhinus treadawayi*	EN	Endemic
Igna Flat	*Coladenia igna*	VU	Endemic
Minor Flat	*Coladenia minor*	N/A	Endemic
Ochrace Flat	*Coladenia ochracea*	N/A	Endemic
Palawan Flat	*Coladenia palawana*	N/A	
Semper Flat	*Coladenia semperi*	N/A	Endemic
Pied Flat	*Coladenia similis*	N/A	Endemic
Pteria Flat	*Darpa pteria*	N/A	
Corona Flat	*Gerosis corona*	N/A	Endemic
Limax Flat	*Gerosis limax*	N/A	
Yellow Flat	*Mooreana princeps*	N/A	Endemic
Trichoneura Flat	*Mooreana trichoneura*	N/A	
Polygon Flat	*Odina cuneiformis*	N/A	Endemic
Chestnut Angle	*Odontoptilum abbreviata*	N/A	Endemic
Corria Angle	*Odontoptilum corria*	N/A	Endemic
Chestnut Angle	*Odontoptilum helias*	N/A	
Banded Angle	*Odontoptilum pygela*	N/A	
Leptogram Flat	*Semperium leptogramma*	N/A	Endemic
Large Snow Flat	*Tagiades gana*	N/A	
Common Snow Flat	*Tagiades japetus*	N/A	
Straight Snow Flat	*Tagiades parra*	N/A	
Trebellius Flat	*Tagiades trebellius*	N/A	
Ultra Snow Flat	*Tagiades ultra*	N/A	
Obtuse-winged Angle	*Tapena thwaitesi*	N/A	

▪ FURTHER INFORMATION ▪

SUBMISSION OF RECORDS
Simple documentation such as taking pictures or writing down notes on the species you find in forests or in your garden will help in the Philippines' ongoing biodiversity database. The Philippine Lepidoptera Butterflies and Moths, Inc. (PhiLep) is a long-term documentation of Philippine butterflies and moths throughout the country, and most of the documentation was produced by citizen scientists. New locality records and ranges of Lepidoptera have been documented by the organization. You can submit your documentation to its website at https://philippinelepidopt.wixsite.com/butterflies. Here are some tips on how to do simple data gathering:

Information on site The specific spot or area where a butterfly was seen is essential for distributional records. This includes the island, province, city, town and barangays.

Date and time It is important to take note of the date when the butterfly was seen, since this may tell us whether it is seasonal or flies all year round. The time reveals if it has time preferences for its occurrences or flight.

Habitats The types of habitat where a butterfly was seen will help in the understanding of its habitat preferences. Some species are sensitive to other habitat types. Forest-dwelling species, for example, definitely prefer to fly in forested areas. Habitats can include grassland, cultivated or agricultural land, and urban, suburban or coastal areas.

Notes on colours The first thing you will notice when you see a butterfly is its colouration. Some species can just have plain colours, while others have metallic colouration that flashes when flying. Simple observation on the colour of a butterfly can help conservationists and biologists determine preliminary identification.

Host plants/larval hosts Depending on the species, caterpillars (larvae) can feed on one plant or several, while some species feed on aphids. Documentation on the caterpillar and the plant it was seen feeding on is essential for the conservation of butterflies. The caterpillars need these specific plants to complete the butterflies' life cycles (to reach adult stage). The plants thus also need to be conserved and preserved.

IMPORTANT WEBSITES
Here are some helpful websites for Philippines butterflies, or similar species in Asia and Southeast Asia:

Badon, J. A. T., Lahom-Cristobal, L. & Talavera, A. A. (Chief Editors). 2012. Illustrated lists of Philippines Butterflies. https://philippinelepidopt.wixsite.com/butterflies

Kunte, K., Sondhi, S. & Roy, P. (Chief Editors). 2021. *Butterflies of India, v. 3.06*. Indian Foundation for Butterflies. www.ifoundbutterflies.org

The Butterflies of Singapore file://localhost/. https::butterflycircle.blogspot.com
Robinson, G. S., Ackery P. R., Kitching, I. J. Beccaloni, G. W. & Hernández, L. M. 2010. HOSTS – A Database of the World's Lepidopteran Hostplants. Natural History Museum, London www.nhm.ac.uk/hosts. (Accessed 18 August 2010).

Learn about butterflies. www.learnaboutbutterflies.com

REFERENCES
Badon, J. A. T. 2014. *Butterflies of the Philippines Field Guide*. Mariposa Press. FL, USA.
Bascombe, M. J, Johnston, G. & Bascombe, F. S. *The Butterflies of Hong Kong*. Academic Press. San Diego, CA, USA.
d'Abrera, B. 1982. *Butterflies of the Oriental Regions. Part I. Papilionidae, Pieridae & Danaidae*. Hill House. Melbourne.

d'Abrera, B. 1985. *Butterflies of the Oriental Regions. Part II. Nymphalidae, Satyridae & Amathusiidae.* Hill House. Melbourne.

d'Abrera, B. 1986. *Butterflies of the Oriental Regions. Part III. Lycaenidae & Riodinidae.* Hill House. Melbourne.

De Jong, R. & Treadaway, C. G. 2007. Hesperiidae of the Philippine Islands. In: Bauer, E., & Frankenbach, T., *Butterflies of the World.* Supplement 15. Keltern (Goecke & Evers).

De Jong, R. & Treadaway, C. G. 2008. Hesperiidae I, Hesperiidae of the Philippine Islands. In: Bauer, E., & Frankenbach, T., *Butterflies of the World*, 29. Keltern (Goecke & Evers).

Ek-Amnuay, P. 2012. *Butterflies of Thailand.* Amarin Printing and Publishing Public Co., Ltd.

Frankenbach, T. *Butterflies of the World*, 37. Keltern (Goecke & Evers).

Igarashi, S. & Fukuda, H. 1997. *The Life Histories of Asian Butterflies Vol. I.* Tokai University Press. Tokyo.

Igarashi, S. & Fukuda, H. 2000. *The Life Histories of Asian Butterflies Vol. II.* Tokai University Press. Tokyo.

Nitin, R., Balakrishnan, V. C., Churi, P. V., Kalesh, S., Prakash, S. & Kunte, K. 2018. Larval host plants of the butterflies of the Western Ghats, India. *Journal of Threatened Taxa* 10 (4): 11495–11550.

Page, M. G. B. & Treadaway, C. G. 2003. Papilionidae IX, Papilionidae of the Philippine Islands. In: Bauer, E. & Frankenbach, T. *Butterflies of the World*, 17. Keltern (Goecke & Evers).

Parsons, M. 1998. *The Butterflies of Papua New Guinea, Their Systematics and Biology.* Academic Press. London.

Schroeder, H. G, & Treadaway, C. G. 2005. Nymphalidae IX, Amathusiini of the Philippine Islands (Nymphalidae: Morphinae). In: Bauer, E. & Frankenbach, T. *Butterflies of the World*, 20. Keltern (Goecke & Evers).

Schroeder, H. G. & Treadaway, C. G. 2005. Eine weitere Unterart von *Delias nuydaorum.* Schroeder 1975 von Sud-Mindanao, Philippinen (Lepidoptera: Pieridae). *Nachr. Entomol. Ver. Apollo N.F. 26* (1/2): 15–16.

Treadaway, C. G. 2012. Nymphalidae XXI, *Euploea* of the Philippines. In: Bauer, E. & Frankenbach, T. *Butterflies of the World*, 37. Keltern (Goecke & Evers).

Treadaway, C. G. & Schroeder, H. G. 2009. A study of the subspecies of *Cethosia biblis* (Drury 1773) from the Philippines (Lepidoptera: Nymphalidae). *Nachr. Entomol. Ver. Apollo N.F. 29* (4): 193–198.

Treadaway, C. G. & Schroeder, H. G. 2012. Revised checklist of the butterflies of the Philippine Islands (Lepidoptera: Rhopalocera). *Nachrichten des Entomologischen Vereins Apollo* Supplement 20.

Triplehorn, C. A. & Johnson, N. F. 2008. *Borror and Delong's Introduction to the Study of Insects* (7th edn). Brooks/Cole, Cengage Learning. CA, USA.

Tsukada, E. & Nishiyama, Y. 1982. *Butterflies of the South East Asian Islands Vol. I. Papilionidae.* Kosaido. Tokyo.

Tsukada, E., Yata, O. & Morishita, K. 1985. *Butterflies of the South East Asian Islands Vol. II. Pieridae & Danaidae.* Kosaido. Tokyo.

Vane-Wright, R. I. & de Jong, R. 2003. The butterflies of Sulawesi: annotated checklist for a critical island fauna. *Zoologische Verhandelingen* 343: 1–267.

ACKNOWLEDGEMENTS
The author would like to acknowledge and thank the following individuals for allowing him to use their photos for the book: Leana Lahom-Cristobal, Agnes Adique Talavera, Linda Alisto, Jojo De Peralta, Leif Gabrielsen, Chris and Ana Chafer, Jean Henri Oracion, Jason Apolonio, Albert Kang, Forest Jarvis, Jonet Carpio, Gerson Kim Penetrante, Adrian Constantino, Harvey Salaga, Fernando Panuculan, Andrea B. Agillon, Noel Buensuceso, Tristan Senarillos, Romana Delos Reyes, Cristy Burlace, Leni Sutcliffe, Reggie Villahermosa, Veronica Prudente, Johnny Corcha and Shekai Alaban.